ISLAM

A poetry reading

Seventh-century coin, minted
when the Umayyad dynasty
ruled from Damascus, Syria

Water pitcher presented to Charlemagne by
eighth-century caliph, Harun al-Rashid

Arabic quadrant, for
measuring the height of
stars, with instructions

Mosque finial of
Selimiye Mosque,
Turkey

Lute decorated with
traditional Islamic patterns

Star lantern

Map of the world by
Moroccan-born writer and
geographer, Al-Idrisi
(1099–1180)

Guidebook to the *hajj* (the pilgrimage)

ISLAM

Written by
PHILIP WILKINSON

Editorial consultant
BATUL SALAZAR

The Qutb Minar,
Delhi, India

Bedouin wearing
traditional costume

Prayer beads

Ubudiah Mosque, Malaysia

Thirteenth-century book illustration
of Ramadan procession

Gold bracelet

Islamic star-shaped
decorative tile

A book rest supporting
a copy of the Qur'an

Sixteenth-century painting
of Muslim astronomers

Bronze bird from Persia

Traditional silk costume
from China

Two of the Rightly Guided Caliphs,
Companions of the Prophet

Tenth-century Arabic copy of a
herbal encyclopedia by Greek
surgeon Dioscorides

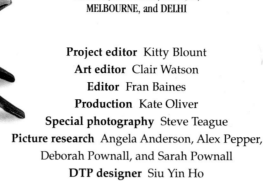

DK

LONDON, NEW YORK, MUNICH,
MELBOURNE, and DELHI

Project editor Kitty Blount
Art editor Clair Watson
Editor Fran Baines
Production Kate Oliver
Special photography Steve Teague
Picture research Angela Anderson, Alex Pepper,
Deborah Pownall, and Sarah Pownall
DTP designer Siu Yin Ho
Jacket designer Dean Price

This Eyewitness ® Guide has been conceived by
Dorling Kindersley Limited and Editions Gallimard

First American Edition, 2002
03 04 05 10 9 8 7 6 5 4 3

Published in the United States by
DK Publishing, Inc.
375 Hudson Street
New York, New York 10014

A catalog record of this book is available from
the Library of Congress.
ISBN 0-7894-8870-1 (plc)
ISBN 0-7894-8871-X (alb)

Color reproduction by Colourscan, Singapore
Printed in China by Toppan,

See our complete
product line at
www.dk.com

A caravan of pilgrims, including a camel
carrying a pavillion called a *mahmal.*

Saudi Arabian
woman wearing a
face veil

Coffeepot

Contents

Mamluk mosque lamp

Early Arabia

THE ARABIAN PENINSULA is home to the Arab people. There had already been advanced cultures in this area before the birth of Muhammad, the Prophet of Islam, in the sixth century. Arabia's position at a crossroads between Asia, Africa, and Europe allowed many Arabs to make fortunes trading. Although most of the Arab tribes worshiped their own idols, Christians, Jews, and followers of Abraham worshiped One God. When Muhammad told them that the religion of the One God had been revealed to him and that at last they had a message, the Qur'an, in their own language and a religion called Islam, some were enthusiastic.

SOUTH ARABIC INSCRIPTION
The Sabaeans, who ruled southern Arabia between the eighth and second centuries BCE, used a script called South Arabic. Archaeologists have found many inscriptions in this angular script, which passed out of use after the Sabaeans lost power.

DATE HARVEST
Settlements grew up at the small oases that are dotted around the Arabian Peninsula. Here there was a reliable water supply and date palms grew, providing a succulent harvest for the local people.

DESERT DUNES
Much of Arabia is desert – either vast expanses of sand with rolling dunes or the desert of black volcanic rocks around the city of Mecca. The name Arab means "nomad" because, in such an environment, many Arab people adopted a nomadic way of life in order to survive.

PETRIFIED FOREST
The Arabian Peninsula is, for the most part, an inhospitable terrain of desert and harsh landscapes, such as these jagged rocks. The most fertile area is Yemen, which gets monsoon rains from the Indian Ocean.

WOMAN FROM PALMYRA
The city of Palmyra in the Syrian desert was built where several trade routes met. Its people became rich because they charged merchants a tax when they passed through. This Palmyra woman is displaying her wealth in the form of gold jewelry.

THE ARAB WORLD

The Arabian Peninsula lies between the Red Sea and the Persian Gulf. The Arab peoples built towns in the fertile area of Yemen, at oases, and on the coasts. To the northeast, the Sasanid Empire of the Persians occupied Iran. To the northwest lay the Christian Byzantine Empire.

The Arab world at the time of the birth of the Prophet Muhammad in 570

Altar for burning frankincense

PRECIOUS PERFUME

Frankincense was one of Arabia's most prized products, and it was widely traded. Trade routes crisscrossed the peninsula and many of the area's early cities, such as Ma'rib and the Nabatean town of Petra (in modern Jordan), grew up along the roads. Trade has been vital to the area ever since.

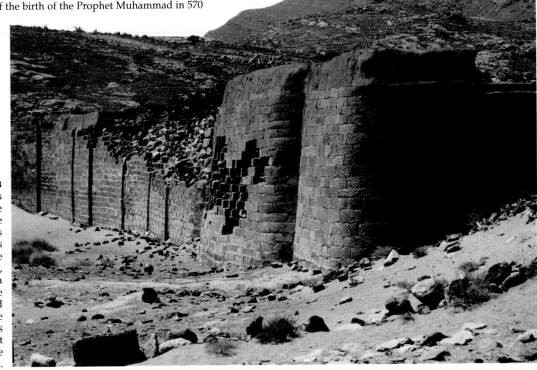

WALLS AT MA'RIB

Ma'rib, in Yemen, was the capital city of the Sabaeans, and some of its ancient walls survive. Ma'rib was built on a trade route and grew into a large, thriving city, with a palace (home of the Queen of Sheba) and many houses. There was also a famous dam, an amazing feat of engineering for the seventh century BCE.

The Prophet Muhammad

MUHAMMAD WAS BORN IN 570 in the city of Mecca (in what is now Saudi Arabia). He was a member of the Quraysh tribe. Orphaned as a boy, he was brought up by his grandfather and uncle. His mission as Prophet of Islam began in 610, when the Qur'an was first revealed to him. Three years later, Muhammad began to preach. He attracted some followers, but his teachings about the one God were not widely welcomed in Mecca, where most of the people worshiped idols, many different pagan gods. Eventually he moved to the city of Medina, which became the center of a great Islamic civilization.

ARCHANGEL GABRIEL
The Qur'an (pp. 10–11) was revealed to Muhammad by the archangel Gabriel, the angel of revelation. On an occasion known as the Night of Destiny, the revelation began. Then the Qur'an was communicated in small parts over a number of years.

WRITTEN OR SPOKEN
This calligraphy represents the name of the Prophet, Muhammad. According to tradition, he actually has 200 names, including Habib Allah (Beloved of God) and Miftah al-Jannah (Key of Paradise). When referring to Muhammad, Muslims usually add the phrase 'alayhi-s-salam (peace be upon him).

The word "Muhammad" written in calligraphy

THE LIFE OF A TRADER
As a young man, Muhammad became a merchant, working for a wealthy widow called Khadija. Arabia was crisscrossed with trading routes linking the peninsula with the Mediterranean and the Indian Ocean. Muhammad traveled with camel caravans along these routes and made several trading journeys as far as Syria. Khadija was impressed with Muhammad, and, although she was considerably older than he was, the two married.

JABAL AN-NUR
Jabal an-Nur (the Mountain of Light) a few miles from Mecca, is the place where Muhammad went to meditate. Every year, during the month of Ramadan (p. 15), Muhammad retired to the mountain to pray, fast, and give to the poor. It was on one of these retreats that the Prophet received the first revelation of the Qur'an.

THE PROPHET
Muhammad, whose name is shown here in stylized form, is the Prophet of Islam. Muslims see him as the last of a series of prophets, including Abraham, Moses, and Jesus, all of whom were mortal.

ON THE MOUNTAIN
When visiting Jabal an-Nur, Muhammad stayed in a cave called Hirah, at the top of the rocky peak. The cave, with an opening that faced toward Mecca, was very small, but there was enough space for Muhammad to pray. One of the Prophet's daughters used to climb the mountain to bring him food so that he could stay in the cave for the whole month of Ramadan.

Star pattern based on "Allah" in Arabic script

ALLAH
Allah is the name of the one God in whom Muslims believe and upon whom all life and all existence depends. He is unique and infinitely greater than any thing He has created. The Qur'an says that He is "unbegotten." In other words, He is eternal, having no origin and no end. He is and always will be.

The Prophet's mosque

MEDINA
Muhammad was persecuted in his native Mecca and some of his followers took refuge in Abyssinia (present-day Ethiopia) under the Christian ruler there. In 622, people from the city of Yathrib, later called Medina, to the north of Mecca, invited Muhammad to go and live there. The Prophet and his followers took up the invitation. Their migration, known as the *hijrah*, forms the start of the Islamic era. Eventually Muhammad defeated the pagans and cleared the idols from the Ka'ba, so Islam could flourish in Mecca, too.

Muhammad's face is veiled because Islam does not allow him to be depicted.

The archangel Gabriel

The Buraq

THE NIGHT JOURNEY
One night the archangel Gabriel woke Muhammad and led him to a steed called the *Buraq*, which the Prophet mounted (p. 61). The Buraq carried Muhammad to the "Furthest Mosque" in Jerusalem, from where he ascended to heaven.

MUHAMMAD'S TOMB
The Prophet died in the lap of his favorite wife, 'A'isha, in her apartment near the mosque at Medina. His tomb was built where he died. Later, his close Companions Abu Bakr and 'Umar, the first two caliphs, were buried on either side.

Pattern based on names of the Companions

COMPANIONS
The Prophet's Companions were his closest followers. They listened carefully to his teachings, memorized the Qur'an, and passed it on to others before it was written down.

The Qur'an

IN THE YEAR 610, the archangel Gabriel appeared to the Prophet Muhammad and through Gabriel, Allah began to reveal the Qur'an, the holy book of Islam. This continued for 22 years. Muslims believe that the Qur'an, Allah's final revelation to humanity, completes the sacred writings of the Jews and Christians, but is on a higher level because its text consists of Allah's actual words. Ever since the Qur'an was revealed, Muslims have preserved its words, first learning them by heart, and later also writing them down. They aim to live by the Qur'an.

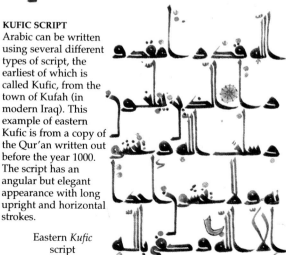

QUR'AN CONTAINER
This beautiful inlaid box is designed to contain a copy of the Qur'an divided into 30 sections. One section is read on each night of Ramadan, the month of fasting, a time when the Qur'an is read intensively.

Bold Kufic script

DECORATED QUR'AN
This copy of the Qur'an is open at the beginning of one of its 114 chapters, or *suras*. Each *sura* has a name that comes from a notable word that occurs in its text.

This box gives the number of verses in the sura. The box at the top gives the name of the sura.

KUFIC SCRIPT
Arabic can be written using several different types of script, the earliest of which is called Kufic, from the town of Kufah (in modern Iraq). This example of eastern Kufic is from a copy of the Qur'an written out before the year 1000. The script has an angular but elegant appearance with long upright and horizontal strokes.

Eastern Kufic script

"Praise belongs to Allah, the Lord of the worlds, the Merciful, the Compassionate, the Master of the Day of Judgment. Thee only do we serve; to Thee alone we pray for help. Guide us on the straight path, the path of those whom Thou hast blessed, not of those against whom Thou are wrathful, nor of those who are astray."

SURA AL-FATIHA, OPENING CHAPTER, THE QUR'AN

The text on this page
is the opening chapter,
Sura al-Fatiha, *which is*
translated below to the left.

ON A GEMSTONE
In the eyes of a Muslim, this
gemstone (below) has been made
far more valuable as it has a
Qur'anic inscription on it, which
is translated below.

"Allah – there is no god but He,
the Living, the Everlasting.
Slumber seizes Him not, neither
sleep; to Him belongs all that is
in the Heavens and the Earth..."

AYAT AL-KURSI, THRONE VERSE, THE QUR'AN

TILE AND TEXT
All over the Muslim
world, beautifully
written quotations from
the Qur'an are used for
artistic decoration.
Muslims everywhere
learn Arabic, the
language of the Qur'an.
This shared knowledge
brings together Muslims
from all countries and
backgrounds.

MUSHAF
When people talk about
"the Qur'an," they are
usually referring to a
book that has the Qur'an
written in it. However,
originally the Qur'an was
recited only and Muslims
learned it by heart. Later,
it was written down and
the written version was
called a *mushaf*, which
means a collection of
pages. A *mushaf* will
usually indicate whether
each *sura* was revealed
at Mecca or Medina.

WRITING IT DOWN
Copying the text of the Qur'an is
something that must be done with
care and reverence – none of
Allah's words must be altered. To
make a handwritten copy of the
Qur'an like this is an activity of
great religious devotion.

11

The Five Pillars of Islam

"In the name of Allah, the Merciful, the Compassionate."

CRESCENT MOON AND STAR
A crescent moon with a star above it was used as a symbol by the Turks in the 15th century. Since then it has become the symbol of Islam. The words of the *Shahada* in Arabic calligraphy have been used here to form the shape of the moon. The words, "In the name of Allah, the Merciful, the Compassionate," make the star.

SHAHADA
The Muslim profession of faith is called the *Shahada*. The English translation of it is: "There is no god but God; Muhammad is the messenger of God." Muslims use the Arabic word for God, which is "Allah." When Muslims use the term Allah, they are referring to the same God that is worshipped by Christians and Jews. The words of the *Shahada* are heard often in the Muslim world because they are repeated during the call to prayer. The *Shahada* is normally whispered in a Muslim baby's ear at birth and at the time of death.

THERE ARE FIVE FUNDAMENTAL requirements of Islam, called the Five Pillars of Islam. The first and most important is the profession of faith. Islam, which means "submission" and comes from the word "peace," is considered by Muslims to be a restating of the same truth – belief in the one God – that was revealed to the Christians and the Jews. This faith was revealed through all God's prophets, including Moses and Jesus, or Musa and 'Isa as they are known in Arabic. Muslims believe that God's final and most universal message was revealed to the last of the prophets – the Prophet Muhammad. Faith in this one God is the basic belief of the Islamic religion. The remaining four Pillars of Islam require all Muslims to be committed to prayer, almsgiving, fasting, and the pilgrimage to Mecca.

Prayer

Muslims must pray at five set times during the day. These regular prayers, known as *salah*, make up the second Pillar of Islam. Muslims may pray on their own or in a group, but every Friday at midday, Muslim men are required to gather together for *salat al-juma'a*, or Friday prayers. Friday prayers are led by an imam (literally "one who stands in front"), who will also give a sermon, or *khutba*.

All members of the community are considered equal in the eyes of Allah so they all perform the same rituals of ablution and prayer.

RISE UP FOR PRAYER
Five times each day the *adhan*, or call to prayer, is heard in Muslim communities. The times for prayer are between first light and sunrise (*fajr*), just after noon (*zuhr*), in late afternoon (*'asr*), after sunset (*maghrib*), and evening (*'isha*). The traditional practice is for someone to make the call from the minaret. The first muezzin was Bilal, a freed black slave, chosen for his fine voice.

PREPARING FOR PRAYER
Before prayer, a Muslim must prepare by ridding the mind of distracting thoughts and by cleansing the body. Ritual washing is normally done using running water – either at the fountain at the mosque or using a tap and basin in the home. In places where there is no water, such as the desert, Muslims may use sand or a stone for ritual cleansing.

IN THE DIRECTION OF MECCA
Because Muslims face the Ka'ba in Mecca during prayers, they need to know the direction, *qibla*, of the city. In the Middle Ages, people made instruments to determine the direction. In mosques, a niche, *mihrab*, in the wall indicates the direction of Mecca.

Qibla indicator

PRAYER BEADS
Allah is referred to in many different ways, known as *al-asma al-husna*, meaning the 99 beautiful names. Many Muslim names, such as 'Abd al-Rahman, servant of the Merciful One, are based on one of these names. The string of 99 beads, like a rosary, that a Muslim uses in private prayer, is a reminder of the 99 Divine names.

PRAYER MAT
The majority of Muslims pray on a mat, and some people take this with them wherever they go, so that they are always able to use it. Prayer rugs are often beautifully made, but any mat, from a silk rug to a piece of reed matting, may be used. It is also permissible to pray on the uncovered ground, provided that it is clean.

Prayer beads may be used to repeat the 99 beautiful names, or to repeat other phrases used in prayer.

Iranian prayer mat

1 THE RAK'A BEGINS
The words Allahu Akbar – Allah is greater (than all else) – open the *rak'a*. Then Allah is praised, and the first *sura*, or chapter, of the Qur'an, called *al-Fatiha* – the Opening – is spoken, together with a second *sura*.

2 BOWING DOWN
When another passage from the Qur'an has been recited, the worshipper bows down, to show respect for Allah. This motion, called *ruku'*, is followed by *qiyam*, standing and praising Allah.

3 PROSTRATION
This position, known as *sujud*, shows the Muslim's humility. The worshipper says silently, "Glory to my Lord the Most High. Allah is greater."

4 SITTING
This seated position, called *julus*, gives the opportunity for a short silent prayer. Then the prostration is repeated. The sequence concludes with a short prayer for the community of Muslims and for the worshipper's sins to be forgiven.

5 PEACE
The final stage is called *salam*, or peace. The person looks to left and right, and then says, "Peace be with you and the mercy of Allah." These words are addressed to all present, seen and unseen.

Stages of prayer

Prayer is performed following a precise order of words and motions. Each unit of this order is called a *rak'a* and is composed of several stages. During prayers the *rak'a* is repeated two, three, or four times – the exact number depends on which of the five daily prayers is being performed.

13

Continued on next page

Almsgiving

The giving of alms (gifts) to the poor and needy is very important in Islam. Of all the ways in which one can give to the poor, the most formal is by paying a tax called *zakat*, which is one of the Five Pillars of Islam. The amount of *zakat* that a person has to pay is worked out as a percentage of their wealth. The tax is distributed among the poor and may also be used to help other needy members of society.

WATER SUPPLY
In addition to paying *zakat*, a person may make other personal donations to help the community. These can provide useful facilities such as this public drinking fountain in Istanbul, Turkey. Many Muslim countries are in dry areas where water can be hard to come by, so giving money for a fountain is especially useful.

PUBLIC BATHS
Hygiene is very important in Islam, and baths are a common sight in towns in Muslim countries. They are often paid for by donations. A typical public bath has a changing room, often roofed with a shallow dome, connected to a series of rooms at different temperatures. The hottest of all is the steam room, where the bather works up a sweat before being cleaned and massaged.

HOSPITALS
The places where the sick are treated are another group of facilities that have been paid for by almsgiving. This beautiful latticed window is part of a hospital originally financed with almsgiving contributions. Medicine was one area where the Muslim world made many advances before the West (p. 30).

MONEY OR GOODS
Zakat is commonly paid in money but may also be given in the form of goods. In both cases, rates of payment are laid down, starting at 2.5 percent of a person's wealth. A person's home and other essential items are not counted when determining what they will pay. The word *zakat* means "purification", because it is believed that giving up part of your wealth purifies what remains.

FOR LASTING GOOD
This document details a gift made to the state for good works. This type of gift is known as a *waqf*, and once given, it cannot be reclaimed. Gifts like this go toward the upkeep of mosques and buildings such as hospitals.

FOOD FOR THE POOR
In some parts of Muslim India, large cooking pots, or *deghs*, are used to prepare food outdoors. At the shrine of Ajmer, two *deghs* are used to make food for the needy, and people visiting the shrine make charitable gifts of food for the pots.

A PROPER MEAL
During Ramadan, Muslims break their fast after sunset with a light snack, which may consist simply of a few dates with water. Sunset prayers are followed by the main meal. This is a bigger meal, but should not be too large because Muslims are not encouraged to eat heavily after the day's fast. In addition, the snack should have already taken the edge off a person's hunger, so a simple dish, such as vegetable soup with bread, may be eaten.

JOYFUL PROCESSION
When the great solemnity of the month of Ramadan comes to an end, there may be a procession. This illustration, from a 13th-century book from Baghdad, shows a procession accompanied with trumpets and banners.

Fasting

Muhammad received the first revelation of the Qur'an during the month of Ramadan, and this month has a special significance in Islam. Every day during Ramadan, Muslims fast from dawn to sunset, avoiding food, drink, and sexual relations. Although this fast, or *sawm*, is one of the Pillars of Islam, not everyone has to go without food. For example, those who are too sick to fast, women who are pregnant, and very young children may be excused.

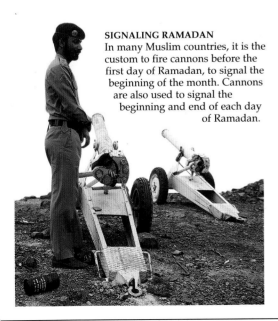

SIGNALING RAMADAN
In many Muslim countries, it is the custom to fire cannons before the first day of Ramadan, to signal the beginning of the month. Cannons are also used to signal the beginning and end of each day of Ramadan.

ENDING RAMADAN
The end of Ramadan is marked by the festival of 'Id al-Fitr – the feast of the breaking of the fast – (p. 60). At the beginning of this festival, the whole community gathers at an outdoor prayer area (or at a mosque) to perform the 'Id prayer. Celebrations last for three days, during which time alms are given to the poor and friends may exchange gifts.

Continued on next page

GUIDEBOOK
An ancient guidebook to Mecca illustrates features of the Sacred Mosque. It shows the stepped *minbar*, from which the sermon is preached (p. 19), together with a hanging lamp.

Tile with the Plan of the Sacred Mosque at Mecca, known in Arabic as the Masjid al-Haram

Quotation from the Qur'an saying that the pilgrimage to Mecca is a duty for all who can make their way there

Pilgrimage

The final Pillar of Islam is pilgrimage, or *hajj*. All Muslims aim to perform this "greater pilgrimage" once in their lives. *Hajj* involves a series of rites that take place annually over several days at the Sacred Mosque at Mecca and the nearby areas of Mina, Muzdalifa, and Arafat. A shorter pilgrimage to Mecca, known as *'umrah*, forms part of the *hajj*, but may be performed by itself at any time of the year.

CLOTHS OF THE KA'BA
The Ka'ba (below) is a stone building, roughly 43 ft (13 m) across, that stands at the center of the Sacred Mosque at Mecca. It is a sanctuary dedicated to God that dates back to the time of Adam. The Ka'ba is covered with a black cloth embroidered with verses of the Qur'an. Every year, the cloth is renewed, and pieces of the old cloth (left) are given away. These fragments are treated with reverence, as is this cloth that once hung inside the Ka'ba.

Piece of cloth from the Ka'ba

AT THE KA'BA
Upon arrival in Mecca, the pilgrims perform *'umrah*, when they circle seven times around the Ka'ba and then pray near the Station of Abraham. In memory of Hagar, the mother of Abraham's eldest son, Ishmael, the pilgrims then run back and forth between two small hills known as Safa and Marwa after drinking water from the well of Zamzam.

HAJJ
After performing *'umrah*, the pilgrims leave Mecca and travel to the valley of Mina. On the second day, they go to Arafat and pray for forgiveness. This is said to give pilgrims a foretaste of the Day of Judgment, when they will rise from the dead, have their souls judged by Allah, and enter paradise if they are worthy. On their way back, they stop at Muzdalifa, where they spend part of the night resting, praying, and gathering small pebbles before returning to Mina. On the third day, they throw seven of the pebbles at the largest of the three stone pillars, which represents the temptations of Satan. For the following two days, the pilgrims stay at Mina and throw further pebbles at the pillars. They must also make an animal sacrifice. They then wash, and clip their hair or shave their heads, to symbolize a new beginning, before returning to Mecca to make the final seven circuits around the Ka'ba.

Rows of arches surrounding the Ka'ba were hung with oil lights. Today the Mosque is lit electrically.

The Ka'ba

The multazam – an area of wall thought to be particularly holy

The Station of Abraham, from which Abraham directed the rebuilding of the Ka'ba

The minbar

The Black Stone

PLACE OF ABRAHAM
The Ka'ba is said to have been founded by Adam, the father of humankind, who is considered by Muslims to be the first prophet. It was rebuilt by Abraham and his son, Ishmael. Set into one corner of the Ka'ba is the Black Stone, a meteorite, said to have been used by Adam when the Ka'ba was first built. The Black Stone was lost, and then found again by Abraham and put in its present position.

PILGRIM'S HOUSE
In some places it is traditional for pilgrims to commemorate their journey by decorating the walls of their houses when they return home. The paintings on this Egyptian house show the pilgrim airplane on which the pilgrim flew to Saudi Arabia, the Ka'ba, and the Grand Mosque at Mecca, and the pilgrim himself, wearing the costume of *ihram*.

IHRAM
Pilgrims must be in a special state of consecration, or holiness, known as *ihram*, achieved by washing and declaring their intention. Male pilgrims wear a simple costume that symbolizes *ihram*. It consists of two large pieces of seamless, unstitched, white cloth.

THE ROAD TO MECCA
This 13th-century picture shows the colorful tents of a group of rich pilgrims. They are on their way to Mecca and have not yet put on the costume of *ihram*. Pilgrims still use tents today. At the time of *hajj*, the area around Mina is filled with thousands of pure white tents. Pilgrims will usually also visit the Prophet's Mosque in Medina during their stay.

The mosque

MOSQUES ARE BUILDINGS that are specifically used for prayer and are open for prayer all the way through the week. In addition, mosques fulfill several other functions in the Muslim community. They provide places where religious discussions can take place, and where education and charitable work can be organized. Most mosques serve their local area and form the spiritual center of the community. They are built and run by local people, though they may be funded by donations from the wealthy. In addition, a town has one main mosque, where Friday prayers are held.

CENTERS OF LEARNING
Many big mosques have libraries, which contain books on religious subjects, including Islamic law. In addition, it is common for mosques to have schools where children learn to memorize and recite the Qur'an.

INSIDE A MOSQUE
Mosques vary enormously in design, from simple plain rooms to vast ornate buildings – there is no one standard design. All that is really needed is a space in which the community can pray and some way of indicating the direction of Mecca. But there are standards of behavior and dress that must be observed inside every mosque. People take off their shoes and cover their heads before going in, and often an area of the mosque is reserved for women.

Model of a mosque

Mosque dome

The mihrab is a niche indicating the direction of Mecca.

Prayer hall

The courtyard is a place to meditate or read.

Prayer hall floor is covered with carpets.

Crescent finial

Entrance to mosque

The call to prayer is given from the minaret.

A fountain or area for washing is found inside.

BRITISH MOSQUE
Mosques are often built in the local style of architecture, like this example in a British city.

STYLES OF MINARET
A minaret is the highest point of a mosque, from which the muezzin traditionally gives the call to prayer (p. 12). Minarets have been built in many different styles. They can be lavishly decorated or plain; square, many-sided, or round; slender or stocky.

Minaret of Sinan's Mosque, Damascus

Minaret of Salihiye Mosque, Syria

Minaret of Giralda, Mosque, Spain

Minaret of Samarra Great Mosque, Iraq

MINBAR

At Friday prayers the congregation listens to the *khutba*, a sermon given by the imam from a raised pulpit called the *minbar*. Some *minbars*, which can be beautifully adorned with inlay and carving, have survived from 1,000 years ago.

OIL LAMP

The traditional way of lighting a mosque was to use oil lamps. These large, hanging lamps could be brightly decorated, like this example of bronze covered with gold and silver, so that they reflected the light and shone more brightly. People who wanted to give alms often made gifts of money for oil for the lamps in their mosque.

15th-century mosque lamp

Mosque finial of Selimiye Mosque in Turkey

Elaborate tile decoration

MOSQUE DECORATION

As Muslims prospered, they devoted more of their wealth to their faith, and some mosques were adorned with sumptuous decoration, like these tiles atop a minaret in Turkey. Carpets for the prayer hall were another favorite gift.

BLUE MOSQUE IN ISTANBUL

In 1453, the Ottomans took over Constantinople (modern Istanbul). The Christian churches there were lavishly decorated and roofed with domes. Ottoman architects built their mosques in a similar style. One of the greatest is the Sultan Ahmed Mosque, known as the Blue Mosque because of its blue-tiled interior.

SYDNEY MOSQUE

The first Muslims to reach Australia were Afghan and Punjabi camel drivers, arriving between 1867 and 1918 to provide essential outback transportation services. Many more Muslims arrived during the late 20th century.

AFRICAN MOSQUE

The earliest mosques had more simple designs, like this 16th-century mosque in Africa. Domes and intricate decoration developed later. The nature of the building, however, is not significant in a mosque. Its function as a meeting place to pray is the most important thing.

The caliphate

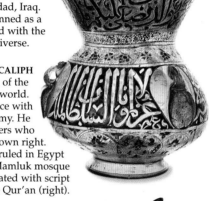

I₊ 632, THE PROHET MUHAMMAD died leaving no obvious successor, so prominent Muslims came together to choose a leader. They elected Abu Bakr and gave him the title *khalifa* (caliph), which means "successor" or "viceroy." Some people thought that the right candidate was 'Ali, the Prophet's cousin, who had married Fatima, the Prophet's daughter. Those who favored 'Ali as caliph became known as Shi'i Muslims, "supporters" of 'Ali. In 656, 'Ali became caliph, but Muslims were still divided about how the caliph should be chosen. Sunni Muslims supported the system of an elected caliphate. Shi'i Muslims believed that the caliphs should be descended from 'Ali and Fatima.

THE ROUND CITY OF BAGHDAD
The first dynasty of Islam was the Umayyad, who ruled from Damascus, Syria. In 749, they were replaced by the Abbasid caliphs who ruled for over 500 years from their capital in Baghdad, Iraq. The city was founded in 763 and was planned as a great circle. This shape, with gates aligned with the compass points, was like a map of the universe.

THE ROLE OF THE CALIPH
The caliph was the symbolic head of the Muslim community throughout the world. He was expected to rule in accordance with Islamic principles and to lead the army. He also gave authority to Muslim leaders who were often very powerful in their own right. The Mamluk sultanate, for example, ruled in Egypt until the 16th century. This is a Mamluk mosque lamp. Such lamps were often decorated with script from the *Sura al-Nur* of the Qur'an (right).

> *"Allah is the Light of the Heavens and the Earth; the likeness of His Light is as a niche wherein is a lamp."*
>
> **SURA AL-NUR, LIGHT CHAPTER, THE QUR'AN**

THE FIRST FOUR CALIPHS
Abu Bakr, 'Umar, 'Uthman, and 'Ali were the first four caliphs and are greatly revered. As close Companions of the Prophet, they followed his example. Because of this they are known as the Rightly Guided Caliphs.

Dhu'l-Faqar, the twin-bladed sword of 'Ali

EARLY CALIPH
Representation of living creatures is discouraged in Islam because it is believed that Allah alone should have the divine right of creation. However, this early portrait shows a caliph, in a style imitated from pre-Islamic Persian coins.

CALIPH'S GIFT
Rulers like eighth-century caliph Harun al-Rashid were very powerful. Harun exchanged gifts with Charlemagne, the Frankish emperor who ruled a vast area of Western Europe. He sent Charlemagne this jeweled pitcher, with an elephant.

Repeating calligraphic inscription

Calligraphy reads, "Allah, Muhammad, Fatima, and 'Ali, Hasan and Husayn."

TIRAZ
Some caliphs gave courtiers, ambassadors, and foreign rulers lengths of specially made cloth – *tiraz* – or robes, woven with calligraphy. In particular, this was a custom of the Shi'i Fatimid caliphs (who claimed to be descendents of 'Ali and Fatima) of Cairo. The cloths were inscribed with the caliphs' names, Islamic prayers, or poems, and were highly prized.

SHI'I STANDARD
In 680 at Kerbala, the army of the Umayyad caliph killed Hussayn, son of 'Ali and Fatima. The battle standard (above) was used to mark the point at which the Shi'i army collected before the battle began and was then a focal point for the army. What happened at Kerbala divided Shi'i and Sunni Muslims still more deeply. Today, around one-tenth of all Muslims are Shi'i.

LADEN WITH GIFTS
One of the duties of the caliph was to protect the holy cities of Mecca and Medina, together with pilgrims journeying there. Pilgrims often traveled with camels heavily loaded with gifts.

Inscription proclaiming the unity of Allah

UMAYYAD COIN
Abd al-Malik, one of the Umayyad caliphs, minted this coin when they ruled from Damascus, Syria. After their defeat by the Abbasids, an offshoot of the Umayyad caliphate ruled Muslim lands in the West from Spain.

ATATURK
The last caliphs were the Ottoman rulers of Turkey. In 1923, Turkey's first president, Kemal Atatürk, came to power. He decided to modernize his country and in 1924 he abolished the caliphate.

First conquests

THE FIRST THREE CALIPHS Abu Bakr, 'Umar, and 'Uthman, expanded their territory quickly, creating an empire that eventually stretched from the Arabian Peninsula to Spain. Much land was gained by military conquest, but Islam also spread peacefully into areas where local rulers made alliances with the caliphs. People of other religions living in these areas – Jews, Christians, and Zoroastrians – became known as *dhimmis* (protected people) because they were protected in return for the payment of a tax. Later, other peoples, including Hindus in western India, also became *dhimmis*.

EXPANDING EMPIRE
By the end of 'Uthman's reign in 656, the empire included Arabia, Palestine, Syria, Egypt, Libya, Iraq, large parts of Persia (modern-day Iran), and Sind (modern-day Pakistan). The Umayyad dynasty (661–750) expanded into the rest of North Africa and Spain and pushed eastward.

CROWN OF RECCESUINTH
This crown was worn by an early Muslim ruler of Spain, at the request of his wife, who was a princess of the Germanic people, the Visigoths.

MAP OF JERUSALEM
This mosaic map shows Jerusalem in the sixth century. It must have looked like this in 638 when, during the reign of caliph 'Umar, the Muslims conquered the city. For many centuries, the city's Islamic rulers governed Jerusalem in a way that was tolerant of the Jews and Christians who lived there and regarded it as a holy place.

ROCK OF GIBRALTAR
Muslim forces landed in Spain in 711, arriving first on the Rock of Gibraltar under their commander, a Berber former slave, Tariq, from whom Gibraltar takes its name (Jebel Tariq). By 715, they had taken over most of Spain, settling mainly in the south, and soon their armies were entering France.

MOSQUE AT DAMASCUS
Under the Umayyad dynasty, the city of Damascus in Syria became the capital of the Islamic empire. The Umayyads built the Great Mosque in the early eighth century.

MOSQUE DECORATION
Mosques were built all around the empire, and many were lavishly decorated. This arch, above a doorway at the Great Mosque in Damascus, shows how Muslim stone masons used different marbles, together with inlays and mosaics made of other brightly colored stones.

RUINS OF CARTHAGE
The great North African city of Carthage, first the home of the Phoenicians, had been ruled by the Romans before it became an outpost of the Christian Byzantine empire for a short time. The victim of many battles, in 697–8 Carthage fell to Muslim armies. The native Berber population who lived there soon accepted Islam and joined the westward drive of the Muslim forces.

Roman triumphal arch, Carthage

CHARLES MARTEL, KING OF THE FRANKS
In the eighth century, much of Western Europe was ruled by a Germanic people called the Franks, under their king, Charles Martel. In 732, Charles defeated the Muslim army between Tours and Poitiers, France, which marked the northwestern limit of the Muslim empire. Five years later, he also drove the Muslims out of southern France.

OUT IN FORCE
This image from an early manuscript shows Muslim soldiers gathering near their tents. Soldiers like these, efficient and well disciplined, were greatly feared in Western Europe. They advanced as far as France to conquer areas such as Languedoc and Burgundy.

BATTLE STANDARD
In 1212, Spain saw a battle at Navas de Tolosa, between the Almohads, the local Muslim dynasty, and a Christian army. The Almohads, who marched behind this standard, were defeated, and Muslim power in Spain was weakened.

Scholars and teachers

LEARNING HAS ALWAYS PLAYED a huge part in the Islamic world. A system of education developed in which children learned to memorize and recite the text of the Qur'an at school. When they had mastered this, they could become students at a higher-level school called a *madrasah*. Still more advanced study could be followed at university level. Muslim education has always had a religious basis, and the high standards produced scholars in a range of fields, from mathematics to poetry.

AL-AZHAR UNIVERSITY
Cairo's al-Azhar University was founded in the 10th century and became the world's most famous Islamic university. Renowned for its philosophical and theological scholarship, its name means "the resplendent." Many academic traditions, such as the distinction between graduates and undergraduates, began at al-Azhar.

AVICENNA
The scholar Ibn Sina (980–1037), known in the West as Avicenna, wrote many important books on medicine and philosophy. In both fields, he developed the work of the ancient Greeks.

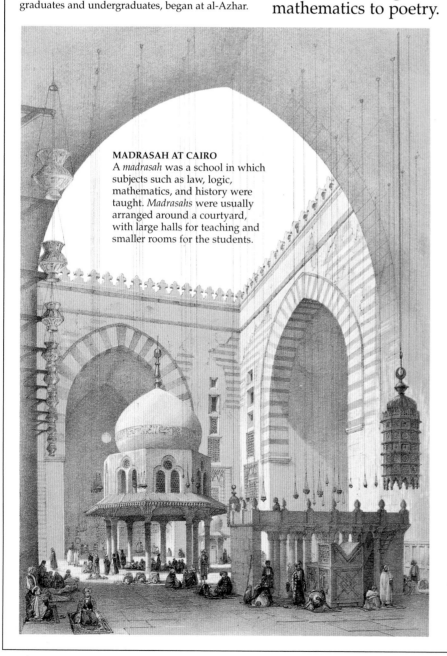

MADRASAH AT CAIRO
A *madrasah* was a school in which subjects such as law, logic, mathematics, and history were taught. *Madrasahs* were usually arranged around a courtyard, with large halls for teaching and smaller rooms for the students.

GLOBE
By the 13th century, Muslim scholars knew a vast amount about astronomy (p. 29). They produced celestial globes like this to show the positions of stars in the sky.

SCHOLAR'S TOMB
Sometimes a famous scholar is commemorated with a large tomb. Bin Ali, a notable scholar of the 14th century from Yemen, was buried in this striking double-domed tomb near Dhofar, Oman.

LIBRARY BOOKS
Centers of learning grew up in big cities such as Baghdad, Iraq, and Damascus, Syria, and these had libraries that were often much larger than the collections in Western cities and universities.

QUR'AN
Arabic scholarship has always been central to Islam. Muslims traditionally learn to recite the entire Qur'an by heart, and they always recite it in the original Arabic, no matter what language they use in everyday life.

LAW BOOK
Muslim scholars produced some very advanced laws. From the earliest times, for example, Muslim women – unlike women in the West – had the right to own and inherit property. This book contains information about how inheritance was calculated.

A MULLAH
A mullah is a person who is learned in religion. Most mullahs have had a formal religious training, but the title can be given to someone with a reputation for religious scholarship.

POETRY READING
Recited or set to music, poetry was important in Arabia even before the time of Muhammad. It continued to be popular. In addition to religious subjects, common poetic themes were love and politics.

Inkpot made of gold and agate

AGATE INKPOT
Calligraphy was an important and respected art. While most writing materials were simple, some very fine pieces, like this 19th century inkpot, were also made.

Continued on next page

Writing

For Muslims, writing is one of the most important of all skills. Because Muslims believe that the Qur'an contains the words of Allah, scribes wish to reproduce those words correctly and with as much beauty as possible. Many Muslims therefore practice calligraphy, the art of beautiful writing. Calligraphy does not only appear in books. It is also used to adorn buildings and other objects, providing decoration that carries a meaning.

EARLY SCHOLARS
This illustration from a 16th-century Persian text shows two children at Qur'anic school. Here they would receive the traditional education of young Muslims, learning to read, write, and recite the text of the Qur'an by heart.

STUDENTS AT WORK
Some Muslim children, like these in Uzbekistan, still attend traditional Qur'anic schools. In many places, modern schooling has replaced this as the main type of education, though children may attend both kinds of school.

Flowing maghribi *script is one popular style of Islamic calligraphy.*

HORSE CALLIGRAPHY
Some Muslim calligraphers can make beautiful pictures using the curving forms of Arabic script. This horse is made up entirely of Arabic script, adorned with different colored inks.

Inscription written in legible form

STONE BANNERS
Calligraphy is used on many Islamic buildings. At this *madrasah* in Konya, Turkey, bands of carved calligraphy curve around the doorway and cross in a knot-like form above it, like fabric banners.

PEN AND INK
Early calligraphers used pens made out of pieces of reed (left), cut to a point with a sharp knife. Black ink was made from soot, mixed with a little water to make it flow.

Animal-hair calligraphy brushes for larger characters

BOOK OF KINGS
This book is an epic poem composed in Iran. It is written in a flowing form of Arabic script called *nasta'liq*. The long curves in the script are said to look like birds' wings.

BOOKBINDER
An Indian craftsman holds the pages of a book together to bind them. Bookbinding became an important craft because of the need to protect copies of the Qur'an.

Animal-hair calligraphy brushes for smaller characters

BROAD-BRUSH EFFECTS
Although a lot of calligraphy is done with pen and ink, an animal-hair brush is another useful tool for broad strokes and for filling in colors between black outlines. These brushes are made with goat and wolf hair.

ARABIAN NIGHTS
The Thousand and One Nights, or *Arabian Nights*, is a collection of stories said to have been told to a king, Shahryar, by his wife Shahrazad. Full of adventure, these magical stories are still entertaining readers today.

27

The spread of learning

ISLAMIC SCHOLARSHIP IS NOT just based on the study of the Qur'an. In a famous saying, Muslim scholars are told to "Seek knowledge, even unto China." In the Middle Ages, there were well-known Muslim scholars in many fields, from astronomy and mathematics to medicine and natural science, and in most areas their ideas were among the most advanced in the world. The Islamic scholars gained much of their knowledge from the ancient world. They translated the works of ancient Greek scholars, preserving information that had been lost or forgotten. The Muslim scholars then built on this with their own original work, carefully recording all their discoveries.

BAGHDAD
Under the Abbasids, the walled city of Baghdad became an important center of learning, with its own university and numerous schools. The city was at its height during the reign of Caliph Harun al-Rashid, who ruled from 786–809. At this time, it was the intellectual center of the Muslim world.

Horseshoe Arch, Cordoba, Andalusia, Spain

ARCHITECTURAL STYLE
Wherever Islamic people have settled for any length of time, they have built using the distinctive Islamic architectural style. These buildings often had simple exteriors which concealed lavish interiors decorated with geometric patterns and calligraphy. The horseshoe arch was also popular because it was elegant and withstood stress and strain well.

Al-Idrisi map showing what was thought to be the shape of the known world in the 12th century

Africa

Arabia

Asia

Unlike modern western maps, south is at the top and north is at the bottom.

Europe

AL-IDRISI
Writer and traveler al-Idrisi (1099–1180) was born in Ceuta, Morocco, but worked for much of his life for the Norman king, Roger II of Sicily. He drew this map of the known world for King Roger and also wrote a book on geography, describing the world north of the equator.

Shaft turned by donkey to operate scoop

Scoop raises water into system of channels through fields

IRRIGATION TECHNIQUES
With water in short supply in many parts of the Islamic world, inventors used their skill to build irrigation devices. These ranged from simple systems, such as this donkey-powered water scoop, to a network of irrigation channels in Iran, which were built underground to reduce loss of water from evaporation. These channels are called *qanat*, and some are 12 miles (19 km) long.

Astronomy

The science of astronomy was important to Muslims because it could be used to figure out the direction of Mecca, so that people knew which way to face during prayers. It also helped them to determine the correct times to pray. As a result, Islamic astronomy became highly advanced. Astronomers developed better instruments, made precise tables showing the movements of the planets, and put together accurate calendars. We are still influenced by these scientists – the names of certain stars derive from Arabic words.

JAIPUR OBSERVATORY
This observatory at Jaipur, India, was built during the 18th century. Many of its instruments are built of stone. These include great curving quadrants, which astronomers used to measure the height of planets as they moved across the sky. The astronomers at Jaipur were successful because they drew on knowledge from both the Arab world and from earlier Indian scientists.

ISTANBUL OBSERVATORY
In 1575, when the Ottoman empire was at its height, the astronomer Taqi ad-Din founded an observatory at Galata (now part of Istanbul, Turkey). This painting of the time shows the astronomers with their equipment, which includes a globe, a sand glass for timing, items for drawing, and all kinds of sighting devices.

Persian astrolabe

ASTROLABE
The astrolabe is an instrument for measuring the height of a star or planet in the sky. It was probably invented by the ancient Greeks, but Muslim scholars and craft workers developed the instrument, making it more accurate and incorporating more data to show the positions of a variety of different stars. It was especially useful to travelers because it could help them to determine their position at sea.

Scales showing the positions of different stars

Central pivot

Rotating arm with pointer

Written instructions for using quadrant

Plumb line

Scale

Arabic quadrant

QUADRANT
This was the simplest instrument for measuring the height of a star. It consisted of a quarter-circle-shaped framework with a scale on the curving part of the frame and a plumb line hanging down vertically. The user looked at a star through a hole in the frame. The height of the star was shown at the point where the plumb line touched the scale.

ASTRONOMY LESSON
This group of scholars is watching as their teacher demonstrates an astrolabe. There were many observatories where lessons like this would have been held. These centers expanded rapidly in the ninth century, during the reign of Caliph 'Abd Allah al-Ma'mun. The caliph founded the House of Wisdom in Baghdad, which included an observatory, and ordered the scientists there to produce more accurate astronomical tables.

Continued on next page

Medicine

Early Islamic medicine was very sophisticated for its time. Doctors knew a great deal about the diagnosis and treatment of diseases, anatomy, childcare, public health, and even psychiatry – and much of this knowledge is still relevant today. Medicine was also well taught, with students traveling thousands of miles to study at famous centers such as Baghdad's 'Adudi hospital.

Title page of the *Canon of Medicine*

CANON OF MEDICINE
The most famous book by scholar Ibn Sina (p. 24) is the *Canon of Medicine*. Ibn Sina based much of this book on the writings of ancient Greek physicians. A huge work, it covers such basic subjects as anatomy and hygiene, describes a vast range of diseases and injuries, and lists hundreds of different medicines.

THE ART OF THE PHARMACIST
The Islamic world produced the first skilled, specially trained pharmacists, who made their own medicines and worked closely with physicians. By the early ninth century, privately owned pharmacies were opening in Baghdad, where a flourishing trade with Asia and Africa provided a variety of medicinal herbs and spices. Pharmacies were soon appearing in other cities.

Ivory handle decorated with a lion head motif

Metal handle decorated with a ram's head

Eighteenth-century surgical knives

UNDER THE KNIFE
The great 10th-century surgeon az-Zahrawi, from Islamic Spain, wrote a book describing techniques such as treating wounds, setting bones, and removing arrows. Not all these operations were painful because Muslim surgeons were the first to use painkillers. Az-Zahrawi designed many types of surgical instruments and similar ones were used for hundreds of years.

Blade folds into handle for safety.

Scalpel

Scissors

Folding handles

BLOODLETTING
Like the ancient Greeks, Muslim physicians believed that bleeding a patient could cure many diseases. Although this practice seems crude today, the early Islamic doctors knew a great deal about blood and how it traveled around the body. One 13th-century Egyptian writer, Ibn an-Nafis, wrote about the circulation of blood, some 400 years before this was "discovered" in Europe.

HERBAL MEDICINE
The ancient Greek surgeon Dioscorides wrote a famous herbal encyclopedia that was translated into Arabic. Its five books describe all kinds of herbs, spices, roots, juices, and seeds that were used to make medicines and other preparations. This page from a 10th-century Arabic version of Dioscorides shows henna, a plant used widely in the Arab world as a dye.

IN STORAGE
Many medicines were made with fresh herbs, but these could not always be found all year round. Herbalists therefore dried leaves, seeds, and other plant parts, so that they were available for use at any time of the year. Herbs were stored in glass or pottery jars, and these were usually sealed with a cork or stopper.

Dark color to keep out light

Pottery storage jars

Pointed blade for piercing and then cutting the skin

Vessel has rounded bottom to aid mixing

Mortar and pestle

WELL-PREPARED
Pharmacists and physicians often prepared medicines by grinding the ingredients together using a mortar and pestle. They made their preparations carefully, often following a standard textbook such as the 11th-century al-Aqrabadhin, which describes many different medications.

Mathematics

Modern mathematics was made possible by Islamic scholars. This was because Muslim mathematicians in Baghdad gathered ideas from both ancient Greece and India, as well as adding contributions of their own. In addition to studying subjects such as arithmetic and geometry, they also founded the science of algebra – a word that comes from the Arabic *al-jabr*, a term describing a method of solving equations.

ARABIC NUMBERS
The numbers we use today began life in India. The Indians used place-value (which gives a value to a number according to its position) and the zero, which was unknown in the West. These ideas, which made arithmetic much easier than before, were in use in India in the 6th century. They were taken up by Muslims by the 9th century and probably passed to Europe in a 12th-century translation of an Arabic book on mathematics.

Indic

Arabic

Spanish

Italian
1 2 3 4 5 6 7 8 9 0

Nomadic or settled

As ISLAM SPREAD, the faith came to people with many different lifestyles. Some were nomads, living in tents and moving from one place to another in search of new grazing lands for their animals. Others lived in settlements that varied from small oasis villages to some of the world's most sophisticated cities. Even town-dwellers were often on the move, for many were merchants, taking caravans of camels across the desert from one market to the next. In this way, both nomadic and settled people helped to spread Islam across western Asia and North Africa.

ON THE THRESHOLD
In Islamic tradition, the door forms the meeting point between the private house interior and the public outside world and may have beautiful carved or painted decoration.

OASIS
Water trapped deep under the ground comes to the surface at oases, small patches of green among the desert's rocks and sand. People can settle here and cultivate crops such as date palms. Oases are also vital water sources for nomadic desert peoples.

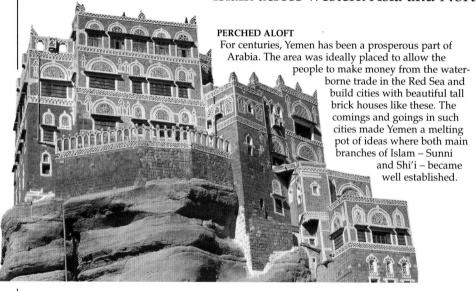

PERCHED ALOFT
For centuries, Yemen has been a prosperous part of Arabia. The area was ideally placed to allow the people to make money from the water-borne trade in the Red Sea and build cities with beautiful tall brick houses like these. The comings and goings in such cities made Yemen a melting pot of ideas where both main branches of Islam – Sunni and Shi'i – became well established.

TRADING PLACES
From Tangier in North Africa to Muscat in Arabia, most Muslim cities have always had markets that formed meeting places for traders all over the Islamic world. Everyone came to trade here – nomads, settled farmers and craft workers, and merchants from near and far. This coming together of peoples made markets prime places for the spread of Islam.

Wooden poles, supported by guy ropes, hold up the tent.

RIDER AND CAMEL
Camels provide ideal desert transportation because they can go for days without food or water, living off the fat in their humps. This one carries tasselled saddlebags beneath a sheepskin saddle blanket. The rider wears traditional Bedouin costume – a long white tunic covered by a sleeveless cloak with a headcloth secured by two woolen coils. These clothes protect him from both sun and wind.

Flat, wide feet do not sink into the sand.

SUPER SADDLE
Horses have always been important to the Arab people, especially those living a nomadic lifestyle. Arabian horses are still widely prized today. This saddle with matching saddle cloth is fit for the finest Arabian horse.

LIVES OF THE MONGOLS
The Mongols of Central Asia, nomads who traditionally lived in round tents called yurts or gers, conquered Islamic lands in the 13th and 14th centuries, after which many Mongols became Muslims.

BEDOUIN TENT
The Bedouins of Arabia and North Africa are desert-dwellers whose traditional life involves nomadic camel-herding. They were among the first to convert to Islam and to spread the faith. Some Bedouin still live in long, low tents, though few are now nomads.

Islamic culture

ISLAM QUICKLY DEVELOPED its own style, which found unique expression in each of the diverse cultures that flourished within its empire. One famous *hadith* (Islamic saying) declares, "Allah is beautiful and loves beauty." Beauty was therefore very important, and the visual arts such as architecture, calligraphy, painting, textiles, metalwork, and ceramics were encouraged. One striking feature of Islamic art is the widespread use of pattern in decoration, inspired by the love of geometry. Poetry and music were among other important forms of art.

FIT FOR A SULTAN
The Topkapi Palace in Istanbul was home to the rulers of the Ottoman empire from the 15th to the 19th centuries. The beautifully decorated private apartments include the dining room of Sultan Ahmet III, adorned with colorful paintings of flower arrangements and bowls of fruit.

BRONZE BIRD
This small statuette of a bird is an example of the metalwork of Persia and dates from the 12th or 13th century. The patterns on the bird's wing and body are typical of the period.

WRITING BOX
Decorated with inlay and calligraphy, this writing box would have belonged to a very wealthy person. It contains pens, knives, brushes, inks, and other equipment for the calligrapher. The superb craftsmanship and luxurious materials of this object show the great importance placed on calligraphy in Islamic culture.

Ivory-handled knives

Brushes

DECORATED QUR'AN
This copy of the Qur'an, made in the 17th century in Delhi, India, has patterns picked out in gold leaf. Not all copies are as richly decorated as this, but when copying the Qur'an, Muslim calligraphers always try to make their script as beautiful as possible.

PATTERNED RUG
The brightly colored patterns on this rug show how Islamic artists adapt shapes and other motifs from the natural world. The design is based on flowers, but they have been simplified, to give them a more abstract quality.

SUFIS

Sufism is the name given today to the spiritual way at the heart of Islam. Those who follow it have their own spiritual practices and a distinctive culture of poetry and music. Sufis aim to discover the inner meaning of Islam. They study under a spiritual teacher in order to come closer to Allah. Their practices sometimes include ecstatic singing and sacred dance rituals that have earned one group of Sufis the nickname "whirling dervishes".

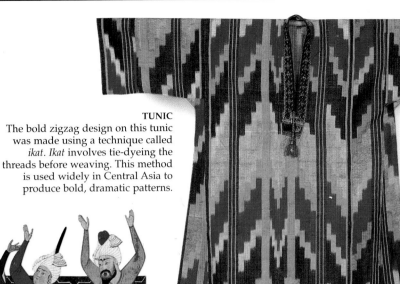

TUNIC
The bold zigzag design on this tunic was made using a technique called *ikat*. *Ikat* involves tie-dyeing the threads before weaving. This method is used widely in Central Asia to produce bold, dramatic patterns.

Five double courses of strings

LUTE
Arab music has its own instruments, and one of the most popular is the *'ud*, the ancestor of the Western lute. The *'ud* is used for both solos and playing in a group of instruments. Its warm sound, and the subtle effects that skilled players can produce, have earned the instrument the title *amir al-tarab* (prince of enchantment).

Inlaid decoration

Pear-shaped body

STAR TILE
Ceramic tiles are a favorite kind of decoration on Islamic buildings. They usually have abstract or calligraphic patterns and can come in intricate shapes, like this star.

The Islamic city

MUSLIMS INHERITED ideas about city planning from early civilizations such as ancient Rome, and they built large cities with facilities that were far in advance of those in Europe. A typical city in the year 1000 would have had a large mosque – usually with a school and library – and a market and baths. There were also caravanseries, which were hotels providing accommodation for traveling merchants and their animals.

Main mosque

City walls

Central square

WATER FOR SALE
Water sellers were a common sight in many Middle Eastern cities before reliable water supplies were installed. They can still be seen in some places.

Metal drinking cups

TOWN PLAN
Houses in an old Islamic city, such as Fez, were tightly packed, but each house had a private courtyard with a small garden and a fountain, as well as a flat rooftop. Many cities, especially in Turkey and Mughul India (pp. 52–53), had public gardens beyond the walls.

SEEKING A CURE
Medicine was advanced in the Muslim world (pp. 30–31) and some Islamic cities became renowned for their able doctors. Travelers would often return home with news of remarkable cures using remedies such as herbs and spices, and spread this knowledge further around the Islamic world and beyond.

MARKET PLACES
Suqs, or covered markets, are usually large, busy places. They are arranged so that shops selling similar goods are close together, so purchasers can compare quality and prices, and so that the official market inspectors (p. 58) can do their job effectively.

THE CITY GRAVEYARD
Burial places were usually outside the city walls. They were pleasant, green spaces with trees, which provided somewhere to walk, meditate, or enjoy the fresh air. Most people had simple graves, marked with a single stone.

Lookout tower gives a good vantage point and firing platform.

Battlements to conceal defenders

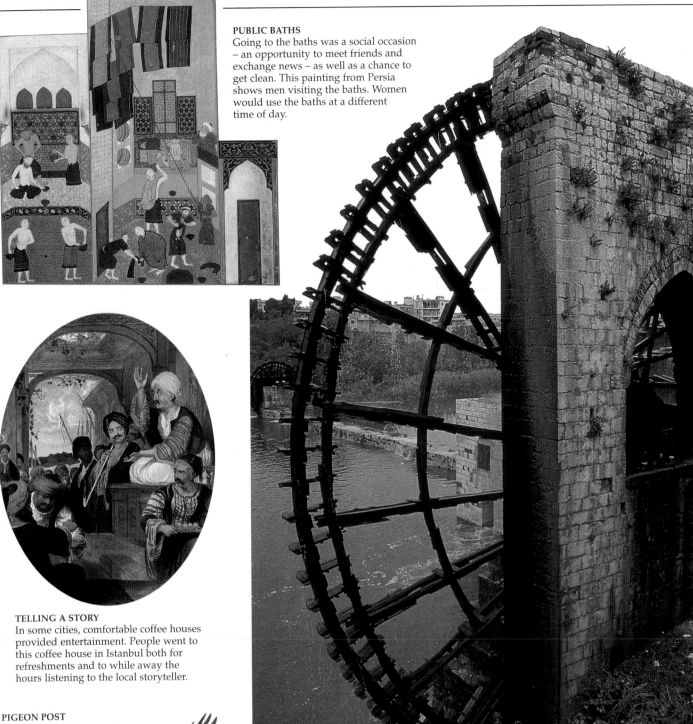

PUBLIC BATHS
Going to the baths was a social occasion
– an opportunity to meet friends and
exchange news – as well as a chance to
get clean. This painting from Persia
shows men visiting the baths. Women
would use the baths at a different
time of day.

TELLING A STORY
In some cities, comfortable coffee houses
provided entertainment. People went to
this coffee house in Istanbul both for
refreshments and to while away the
hours listening to the local storyteller.

PIGEON POST
Major Islamic cities were
connected with an efficient
postal service. Mail
was transported by
camels, mules, or horses,
and in 1150, the Sultan of
Baghdad even started a
postal service using
carrier pigeons.

City walls,
Morocco

CITY WALLS
Walls enclosed many Muslim cities. They had
to be strong enough to keep out attackers, give
somewhere for defenders to stand safely, and
provide a good view of the surrounding
countryside. Gates could be locked to keep out
enemies, or opened, when guards could keep an
eye on who was entering and leaving the city.

WATERWHEELS
Bringing water into the city was sometimes
a major task. In Hamah, Syria, two huge
wooden waterwheels mounted on massive
stone arches were built to raise water from
the river to supply the town. Building wheels
like this required great engineering skill.

Merchants and travellers

TRADE HAS ALWAYS played a key role in the Islamic world. The Prophet himself came from a people who had long ago established the two great caravan journeys from Mecca, the Winter Caravan to the Yemen and the Summer Caravan to the outskirts of the Roman Empire. When Muslim armies took over territory, traders were quick to follow, opening up routes that led east to China, south into Africa, northwest to Europe, and southeast across the Indian Ocean. The faith of Islam was soon spread by merchants as far as Malaysia and Indonesia. Muslims did not only travel for trade, they also went in search of knowledge, on diplomatic missions, and of course to make the Pilgrimage.

IBN BATTUTA
Among the early Muslim travelers, Ibn Battuta, from Tangier (in present-day Morocco), was the most remarkable. Setting out on the Pilgrimage in 1325, he continued traveling, going 75,000 miles (120,000 km) in 29 years. He visited West and East Africa, Arabia, India, and China, and when he returned he told the story of his adventures to the Sultan of Morocco.

MERCHANTS ON THE MOVE
This 13th-century illustration of merchants comes from a book by the writer al-Hariri, who came from Basra, Iraq. Men like these didn't just carry items for sale; they also carried ideas, inventions, and Islam itself, which was often introduced to new areas by merchants who settled far from home.

Silver coins from Baghdad found in a Viking grave in Sweden

COINS FOR TRADE
Archeologists have found out where Islamic traders went by unearthing their coins. The Viking lands, Sri Lanka, and the heart of China are three places where Muslim coins have been discovered. Islamic coins were widely respected because of the high proportion of precious metals they contained. These currencies greatly helped the growth of world trade.

Islamic trade routes

TRADE ROUTES
Official reports, travelers' tales, and archeology have all provided clues about the routes taken by Muslim traders. One route stood out above all – the Silk Road. It was actually a number of roads across Central Asia, linking China and Europe, passing through many parts of the Muslim world on the way.

SALT CARAVAN
This salt caravan is traveling to Timbuktu in Mali (p. 48). Salt was essential for seasoning and preserving food, and early Muslims sold it for vast sums. There were rich sources of salt in Africa, at places such as Taghaza, today in Algeria, where the locals even constructed buildings from salt. From here, caravans carried salt south, and the merchants spread Islam as they traveled.

DHOW
The most common trading vessels in the Indian Ocean were dhows, which are still used today. With their triangular sails, these boats are easy to maneuver and sail in headwinds. Their captains navigated by looking at the stars and many of them also used the magnetic compass. They also had an excellent knowledge of currents, sea-marks, and winds.

Tasseled saddlebag

BACTRIAN CAMEL
With their great staying power and their ability to produce milk on a diet of bitter vegetation and foul-tasting water, camels enabled the Muslims to survive and travel in inhospitable places. The two-humped Bactrian camel was found on the northern routes, the one-humped dromedary in the south.

Ropes help support mast

Furled lateen (triangular) sail

Main mast

CANDY FOR SALE
In countries such as Saudi Arabia, stores and markets have extremely enticing candy counters. For centuries, the Arab world has had a reputation for its confectioneries, and English words such as "sugar" and "candy" come from Arabic.

NOMAD WOMAN SPINNING
This painting shows an Egyptian livestock herder and his wife outside their tent. The woman is spinning wool to make thread. She uses some of this to make clothes for herself and her family. What is left over can be sold at a local market.

Stern rudder

Continued on next page

FRANKINCENSE
A resin from trees growing in southern Arabia, frankincense is burned for its perfume and was also an ingredient in medieval medicines. Frankincense was in great demand in Christian Europe because it was used in religious services. It became a major trading item for Muslim merchants.

NARWHAL TUSKS
Among the marvels on sale in medieval markets were tusks taken from the narwhal, a small species of whale. Stories of the unicorn, the mythical beast with a single horn, fascinated people in the Middle Ages and unscrupulous traders claimed that narwhal tusks were unicorn horns.

HUNTING BIRDS
Nobles in both East and West enjoyed hunting with falcons, and the Arab world produced some of the best, and most expensive, birds. When Muslim envoys visited the Chinese emperor during the Ming dynasty, he asked them to bring him falcons.

Exotic goods

The Muslim world had two enormous business advantages. Muslim merchants had a huge range of contacts over land and sea, so they could trade in everything from African gold and Chinese porcelain to European amber and furs. Muslim craft workers were also highly skilled, so merchants could bring back raw materials, which workers then transformed into all kinds of items – leather goods, metalwork, textiles, glass – that always found a ready market.

COTTON
Grown originally in Egypt and Iraq, cotton was a popular material for clothing because it was cool, comfortable, and cheaper than linen.

Cotton plant

OILS
Used in cooking, for soaps and cosmetics, and in lamps like this, oil was traded widely. The fine plant-based oils of the Muslim world were far more pleasant to use than the smelly fish oil that was often found in Europe.

CAMEL CARAVAN
Before modern forms of transportation appeared, camel caravans, each beast loaded with bags containing trade goods, were a common sight in Arabia, the Sahara, and on the Silk Road across Asia.

SILKS
Muslim merchants brought silk yarns and finished fabrics from China along the Silk Road (p. 38). The yarns were woven into cloth in cities such as Damascus (which gave us the word damask), in Syria, and sold on to Western traders.

Silk fabric

Robe dyed using indigo

DYES
Blue was a very popular color for fabrics and there was a valuable trade in indigo, a blue dye made from plants and used today in clothes such as denim jeans. Other dyes, such as Roman purple made from murex shellfish, were rarer and more expensive.

THE IVORY TRADE
Elephant ivory was brought across the Sahara and through Ethiopia to be exported from the ports of North Africa. Much of it went to Muslim Spain, where craft workers produced stunning ivory objects, such as decorated horns and intricately carved caskets.

Oyster shell with pearl

PEARL FISHING
Diving for pearls was dangerous work, but divers risked their lives in the fine pearl beds of the Arabian Gulf and Indian Ocean because of the huge demand. There were thriving pearl markets in Bahrain, Sri Lanka, and around the Strait of Hormuz, between Oman and Iran.

Pearl necklace

Elephant ivory

Food trade

The Muslim world developed a vigorous trade in various types of foods, and this business still continues today. The trade was beneficial in several ways. Not only was there great financial gain for the merchants, but Western Europe was also introduced to foodstuffs from all over Asia. Without Muslim merchants, Europeans would have had no rice, sugar, or coffee. In addition, the merchants set up trading colonies in many parts of the world, and this helped Islam to spread eastward as far as Southeast Asia.

Thai rice pot

Cinnamon sticks

Peppercorns

RICE
The Muslims brought rice from Southeast Asia and it soon became a popular food in parts of Europe. Later, Western growers learned how to grow rice for themselves.

THE FRUIT TRADE
Muslim travelers introduced new species of fruit, such as the apricot, into Europe. Dried fruit, such as dates, kept for a long time and could be carried for months. Fresh fruit did not travel so well, although highly valued melons were sometimes wrapped in lead to preserve them.

Ginger

Nutmeg

Cherries

Apricots

PRECIOUS SPICES
Grown on the islands of Indonesia, spices fetched high prices in Europe and western Asia, where they were used in both food and medicines. From the time of Muhammad until the 16th century, Muslim merchants ran the spice trade, bringing nutmeg, cloves, cinnamon, and other spices to Arabia by sea and selling them at a huge profit to European traders.

Cloves

Figs

Dates

Bedouin bag for coffee beans and cardamom pods

SUGAR
A great luxury in the Middle Ages, sugar was brought west from Iran and Iraq to Muslim Spain. Access to this expensive ingredient gave Muslim confectioners the chance to create their own specialities – sherbet from Persia, various types of candy, sweets made from the liquorice plant, and Turkish delight – all of which eventually reached Europe through trade.

Sherbet

Tea leaves

Green coffee beans

Boiled candies

TEA AND COFFEE
India and China were sources of tea, while coffee was grown in Yemen and traded from the town of Mocha, which gave its name to a type of high-quality coffee. Both drinks came late to world trade but became very fashionable in the 18th century.

Turkish delight

Liquorice

Sugared almonds

41

The crusades

THE CITY OF JERUSALEM is sacred to followers of three faiths -- Islam, Christianity, and Judaism. From the seventh century, Jerusalem and the surrounding area were ruled by Muslims, who had mostly lived in harmony with the Christians and Jews of the city. But in the late 11th century, the Christian Byzantine Empire, based in Turkey on the pilgrimage route to Jerusalem, was at war with the Muslim Seljuk Turks, and Christian pilgrims reported difficulties in visiting Jerusalem. The Europeans launched a series of largely unsuccessful wars called the crusades to try and defeat the Muslims and take over Jerusalem and other nearby lands.

PREACHING THE CRUSADE
In 1095, Pope Urban II preached at Clermont, France. He called for a Christian army to capture Jerusalem. A number of European lords saw this as an opportunity to create power bases in and around the city.

SELJUK BOWL
In the 11th century, Turkish warriors called the Seljuks, portrayed on this painted bowl, ruled a Muslim empire that stretched from Iran and Iraq to the eastern Mediterranean.

ENGINE OF BATTLE
The crusades involved many sieges when the European armies attacked fortified cities such as Antioch and Damascus. These attacks were often ruthless, bloodthirsty assaults, and the crusaders sometimes used powerful, outsize weapons, like this giant crossbow, when besieging Muslim cities.

Winding mechanism to pull back string

INTO THE BATTLE
In the first crusade (1096–99), a number of French and Norman knights, such as Godfrey of Bouillon, took armies to Jerusalem. After numerous battles with the Muslims, they were able to set up small kingdoms for themselves in the East.

Painting of battling Christians and Muslims

Bolt ready to fire

Handle for aiming crossbow

JERUSALEM
The first crusade ended when Jerusalem fell to the Europeans in July 1099, and Count Baldwin of Flanders was crowned king of the city. Christians remained in power here for over 80 years.

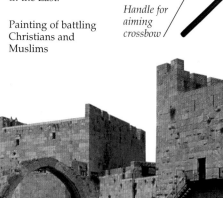

KRAK DES CHEVALIERS

The European knights who occupied the Holy Land during the crusades built impressive castles as military bases. The strongest and biggest of these castles was Krak des Chevaliers in Syria. It was rebuilt by French knights in the early 12th century, and its massive walls kept out many attackers.

Tall tower gives good lookout position

Aqueduct for water supply

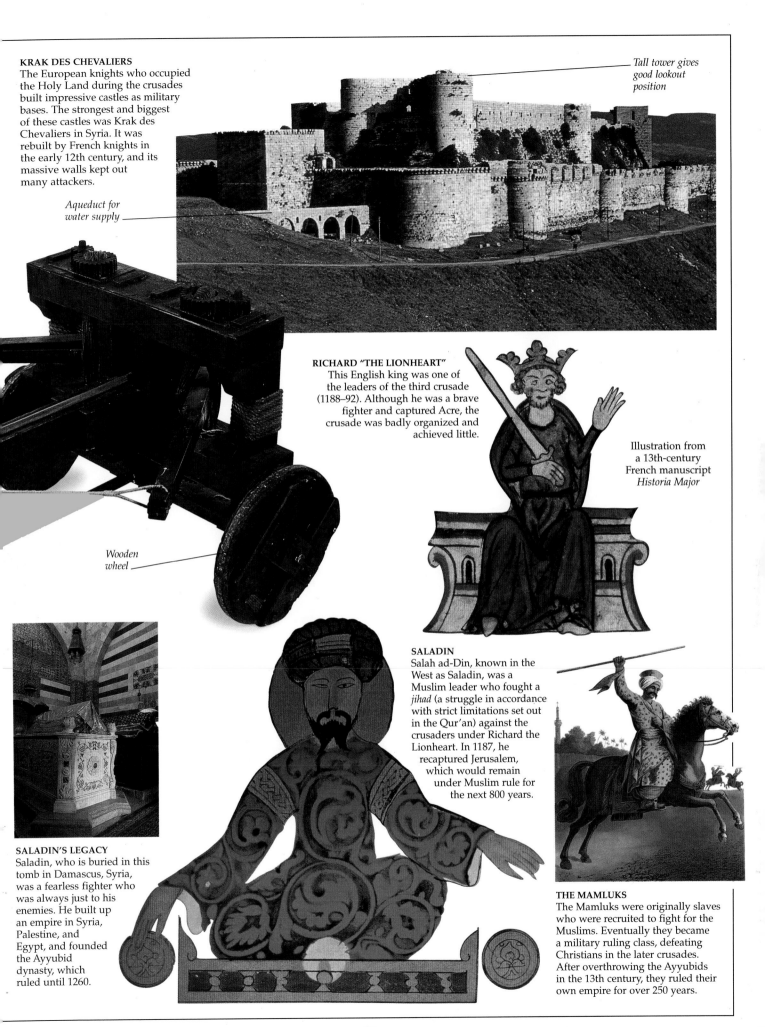

Wooden wheel

RICHARD "THE LIONHEART"

This English king was one of the leaders of the third crusade (1188–92). Although he was a brave fighter and captured Acre, the crusade was badly organized and achieved little.

Illustration from a 13th-century French manuscript Historia Major

SALADIN

Salah ad-Din, known in the West as Saladin, was a Muslim leader who fought a *jihad* (a struggle in accordance with strict limitations set out in the Qur'an) against the crusaders under Richard the Lionheart. In 1187, he recaptured Jerusalem, which would remain under Muslim rule for the next 800 years.

SALADIN'S LEGACY

Saladin, who is buried in this tomb in Damascus, Syria, was a fearless fighter who was always just to his enemies. He built up an empire in Syria, Palestine, and Egypt, and founded the Ayyubid dynasty, which ruled until 1260.

THE MAMLUKS

The Mamluks were originally slaves who were recruited to fight for the Muslims. Eventually they became a military ruling class, defeating Christians in the later crusades. After overthrowing the Ayyubids in the 13th century, they ruled their own empire for over 250 years.

Arms and armor

By THE 11TH CENTURY, Muslims were highly skilled in metal craftsmanship – and this included weapon production. For a fighting man, good arms and armor were often a matter of life and death, so soldiers wanted the best equipment that they could afford. The mounted warriors of the Islamic world used the sword, lance, and mace. Most were also skilled archers. Beautiful and intricate swords, shields, and other weaponry were the envy of the non-Muslim world. However, Muslim armies were also quick to adopt weapons that originated in the West, such as cannons and firearms.

CANNON MINIATURE
By the early 14th century, European armorers were starting to make cannons and these powerful weapons were quickly taken up by Muslim armies. This painting shows cannons being used by Muslim troops at the Siege of Vienna in 1529.

19th-century Indian steel shield with gilt decoration

TURKISH HELMET
This Turkish helmet dates from around 1500. It is made of iron and patterned with silver. It carries the mark of the "Arsenal of Constantinople" (now Istanbul) where the weapons and armor of the Turkish army were held.

SHIELD OF STEEL
The Mongols developed small, round shields made of leather. When enemy archers fired, their arrows stuck in the leather and could be pulled out and reused. Later round shields were made of steel with a curving surface, to protect the user from both bullets and sword blows. Shields like this were popular in India and Iran from the 18th century onward.

Sword and sheath of Shah Tamasp of Persia

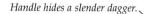

Handle hides a slender dagger.

GRENADE
First used in China, grenades containing gunpowder were used by both Muslims and Christians in the Middle Ages. This 13th-century example was made of clay in Damascus, Syria.

Jambiya (and sheath, below right)

Khanjar and decorated sheath

MACE
Maces were sometimes carried as a sign of rank, but they were also fighting weapons used by mounted warriors. In skilled hands, a mace could break an opponent's bones, even if he was wearing armor.

Steel mace from Persia

KHANJAR
In many parts of the Muslim world it was common for men, and even boys, to carry weapons. This is a 20th-century dagger from Yemen, called a *khanjar*.

JAMBIYA
First made in the Arabian Peninsula, the *jambiya* was a curved dagger. It proved popular – either as a plain fighting dagger or as an ornate ceremonial weapon – and spread all over the Muslim world.

SHOOTING LESSON
Handheld guns first appeared in Western Europe in the 15th century and Muslim soldiers soon began to use them. It was not long before Muslim craft workers started to make such weapons for themselves, often in workshops run by master-armorers from Portugal. In this picture, 16th century Indian Emperor Akbar is learning how to handle one of the latest weapons.

Gold-barreled musket

MUSKET
When they were first imported to the East, guns like this European flintlock musket were resisted by high-ranking Muslim soldiers, who preferred the bow and the curved sword. But when their enemies began to take up firearms, Muslim warriors were forced to do the same, and weapons like the musket were valued all over Asia.

SWORDS AND BATTLE-AXES
The tabar, or battle-ax, was a widespread weapon. Such axes had steel blades and were not always as ornate as this one, which is adorned with silver and gilding. Muslim soldiers also fought with distinctive swords with curved blades that broadened toward the tip. In Europe these were known as scimitars (above).

Spain

MOORISH COIN
The Moors – the name Christians gave to the Muslims from Morocco – brought with them their own coinage and systems of government. After the defeat of the Moors, early Spanish Christian kings continued to use Islamic designs on coins.

DURING THE EARLY EIGHTH century, Muslims from Morocco invaded Spain – soon they controlled most of the Iberian Peninsula. Muslims ruled in Spain until the 15th century, although they never governed the entire peninsula, as Christian kingdoms survived in the north. After the fall of the caliphate in the 11th century, Moorish Spain began to be conquered by the Christians of the north and the east, but southern cities such as Cordoba and Seville were centers of Islamic art and learning.

GREAT MOSQUE AT CORDOBA
Begun in the ninth century and later extended, the Great Mosque, or Mezquita, in Cordoba was a symbol of Muslim power in Spain. It is a dazzling example of Islamic architecture. Over 850 columns of granite, jasper, and marble support a ceiling raised on double arches.

MINSTRELS
The musicians of Muslim Spain were among the best in Europe. Some of them were wandering minstrels who introduced European players to the lute, and to the use of the bow to play stringed instruments.

CALIPH'S BOX
A great Moorish craftsman produced this box during the 10th century. It is inscribed with the name of Al-Mughira, son of 'Abd al-Rahman III, who reunited Islamic Spain after a time of disorder and ruled as Caliph of Cordoba.

Scenes showing pleasures of courtly life

THE ALHAMBRA, GRANADA
In the 14th century, Spain was ruled by the Nasrid dynasty who were based in Granada, in southern Spain. Here they built the great fortified palace called the Alhambra, which means "red palace," after the warm color of its stone. It was designed to represent paradise on Earth and its tall towers and strong outer walls hide luxurious interiors.

ALHAMBRA COURTYARDS
The beauty of the Alhambra lies not only in its exquisite Islamic decoration, but in the clever use of light and water to create a sense of space. Courtyards fill the palace with light, and many have tranquil pools that gently reflect the light. Arched walkways create shaded areas where the Nasrids could walk or relax.

MUDEJAR TOWER
In many parts of Spain, Muslim craftsmen carried on working under Christian rule. They developed a style, now known as *mudéjar*, which used Islamic patterns to decorate brick-built wall surfaces, as in this tower at Teruel.

THE LAST MUSLIM KINGDOM
As the Christians gradually conquered Spain, the Muslim rulers were pushed south. By the 15th century, only the kingdom of Granada, the area in southern Spain around the walled city of the same name, remained in Muslim hands.

THE GARDENS OF THE GENERALIFE
In the Qur'an, paradise is described as a garden – usually an enclosed or shaded garden in which water flows. To escape from the political life of the palace, the Nasrid caliphs created a tranquil garden paradise on their country estate, the Generalife, which looked down over the city of Granada.

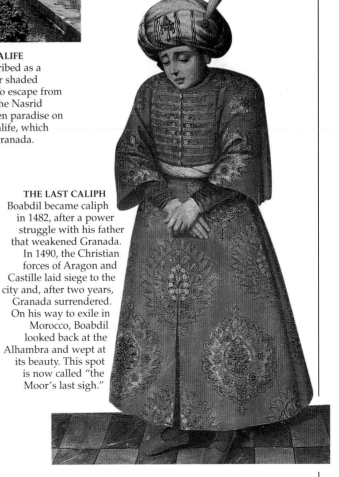

THE LAST CALIPH
Boabdil became caliph in 1482, after a power struggle with his father that weakened Granada. In 1490, the Christian forces of Aragon and Castille laid siege to the city and, after two years, Granada surrendered. On his way to exile in Morocco, Boabdil looked back at the Alhambra and wept at its beauty. This spot is now called "the Moor's last sigh."

MOORISH INFLUENCE
This metalwork decorates a door in the royal palace in Seville. The palace was not built by a caliph but by a Spanish king, Pedro I, and shows the great influence of Islamic art in Spain.

Africa

By THE END OF THE UMAYYAD dynasty of caliphs in 750, Islam had spread across North Africa from Egypt to Morocco. From here, the faith spread southward, as Muslim Berber and Tuareg merchants crossed Africa carrying not just goods, but also ideas. Great cities of Islamic scholarship were established at Timbuktu and Djenne (both in Mali) and Chingetti, in Mauritania. Today Muslims – most of them Sunnis – are in the majority in North and West Africa, and many East African countries. Africa is a vast and varied continent, in which Islam exists side by side with many different local cultures and with political systems that range from socialism to monarchy.

WOMAN WARRIOR
One of the best known accounts of the Muslim conquests in North Africa is an epic called the *Sirat Beni Hilal*. One especially popular character is the heroine Jazia, a warrior who is shown here riding her camel.

BERBER WOMAN
The Berbers are the peoples of the mountains and deserts of North Africa. They are Muslims who have held on to many of their local traditions, such as wearing bright-colored costumes and silver jewelry.

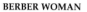

Wide margin allows the pages to be turned without touching the text.

ILLUMINATED COPY OF THE QUR'AN
Calligraphy and other scholarly skills were as highly valued in Africa as in the rest of the Muslim world, and Africa had some famous centers of learning. One of the largest of these was 15th- and 16th-century Timbuktu. Scholars from all over North Africa came to the city's library to consult precious manuscripts like this copy of the Qur'an.

Earth pinnacle built around wooden post

DJENNE MOSQUE
Earth is the traditional building material in many parts of Africa. In addition to being used for houses, large buildings, like this mosque at Djenne in Mali, can be made of earth. Djenne was one of the most important trading centers along the Niger River.

MINARET AT SOUSSE
When the Muslim conquerors took over areas like Tunisia, they founded cities and built mosques in which to pray. The ninth-century mosque at Sousse, with its round stone minaret, is one early example.

WEARING THE QUR'AN
This tunic was worn by a warrior of the Asante people of West Africa. The pouches each contain a text from the Qur'an, which warriors believed would protect them in battle.

Leather pouch containing verse from the Qur'an

TILE PATTERNS
These hexagonal wall tiles from North Africa bear patterns that are based on plant forms. The flowers, leaves, and twining stems have been made into abstract designs in typical Islamic style.

PRECIOUS METAL
The people of West Africa were skilled gold workers before the arrival of Islam. The Muslims put these skills to work to produce gold coinage.

MEMORIZING THE QUR'AN
Islam brought formal education to many parts of Africa for the first time. This Mauritanian student is reading a *sura* (chapter) of the Qur'an, and learning it by heart.

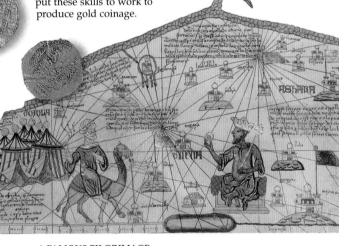

A FAMOUS PILGRIMAGE
Mali was the center of a large West African empire during the 14th century. Its ruler, Mansa Musa, made the pilgrimage to Mecca in 1324–25, and his long journey is recorded on this map.

Smooth outer coating of mud protects walls.

Wooden beams strengthen the structure.

DOMED TOMB
Most Muslims have simple graves, but there is a tradition of building larger tombs for caliphs and other notable people. The small tomb above, near Khartoum in Sudan, was probably built for a local saint. It is marked by a simple dome so that people can visit to pay their respects.

49

Mongols and Turks

In 1219 THE LANDS OF ISLAM were invaded by Mongol armies from the north. By 1258, the Mongols – great warriors from the steppes of Mongolia – had sacked Baghdad and killed the caliph, devastating Islam's political center. But in 1260, the Mongols were defeated by the Mamluks, and many converted to Islam. The next great Muslim power was the Ottoman empire, founded by the Turks in 1290. They conquered part of Eastern Europe and, like the Arabs before them, became the dominant political force in Islam.

GENGHIS KHAN
Genghis Khan was a Mongol warlord who came to power in 1206 when he succeeded in uniting warring Mongol tribes. He then began a campaign of raiding and conquest. At his death in 1227, his empire stretched from China to the borders of Europe.

MONGOL SOLDIER
The Mongol warriors were skilled horsemen and ruthless fighters. Moving at great speed, they killed millions and destroyed hundreds of settlements to bring much of Asia under the control of Mongol rulers.

WARRIOR BOWL
The Mongols were proud of their warriors, as this decorated bowl from the ninth century shows. Because they began as a nomadic people, the Mongols' detailed knowledge of the land meant that they were able to vanish into the countryside, reappearing again suddenly to take their enemies by surprise.

Embroidered cloth

Pillar of skulls

THE NEW MONGOL CAPITAL
After the death of Genghis Khan, his empire was divided between his three sons and his grandson, Kublai Khan. The eastern empire prospered under Kublai Khan, and he founded the Yüan dynasty in China where he built a new capital, called Khanbaliq, now Beijing.

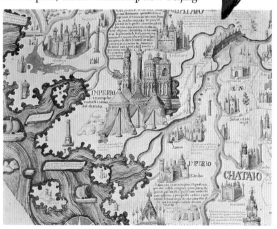

THE RUTHLESS TIMUR
Perhaps the cruelest of all the Mongol conquerors was Timur, or Tamerlane. He was a Turkish-Mongol leader who claimed to be a descendant of Genghis Khan. In the 14th century he conquered much of the western part of the Mongol empire, taking Baghdad in 1390. He liked to display his victims' skulls after major battles and this painting, of his victory at Baghdad, shows a gruesome tower of skulls.

FALL OF CONSTANTINOPLE

Constantinople (modern Istanbul) was the capital of the Christian Byzantine Empire. During the Middle Ages, the Turks took over more and more of this empire, and in 1453, Constantinople itself fell to the sultan Mehmet II. The city became the new center of the Ottoman Empire.

Fortress of Rumeli Hisari, built by Mehmet II as a base from which to attack Constantinople

Recurved bow, the favorite Mongol weapon

Text reads: "Suleiman Shah son of Salim Shah Khan always triumphant."

Tughra of Suleiman I

SIGN OF THE SULTAN

Each Ottoman sultan had a *tughra*, or official signature, specially created for him. It was designed to prevent forgery and could only be used by the sultan's staff. These staff were part of a huge civil service that the Ottomans developed for running their empire. Able civil servants could be promoted and rise to high social rank.

SULEIMAN THE MAGNIFICENT

Suleiman I, known in the West as "the Magnificent" and in the East as "the Lawgiver," ruled with absolute power from 1520 to 1566, when the Ottoman Empire was at its height. Determined to extend the empire, he advanced into Europe and in 1529 he besieged Vienna, in Austria. Despite his powerful army, he failed to capture Vienna.

Suleiman 1

THE CONQUEROR

Ottoman Sultan Mehmet II, was known as "the Conqueror," after his capture of Constantinople in 1453. He was a broadminded man, interested in all types of culture. His court attracted scholars and craftsmen from all over the Muslim world and he had his portrait painted by the Italian artist Bellini.

Central Asia, Iran, and India

BURNING BRIGHT
The Ghaznavids, whose craftsmen made elaborate metalwork like this lamp, were Seljuk rulers who controlled Afghanistan and much of Iran. They were at the height of their power in the early 11th century. The Ghaznavids were Sunni Muslims who opposed the rival Shi'i dynasty, the Buyids, in Iran.

Pierced decoration

Lamp is made of cast bronze

ISLAM CAME EARLY TO IRAN, an area that was completely conquered by Muslim rulers by the year 641. In the following centuries, a series of ruling dynasties reigned in Iran, including the Seljuks from Turkey, the Mongols from Central Asia, the Timurids (the dynasty of the war leader Timur), and the Safavids. India was also a region of huge variety, with many different religions. Muslims – from the first conquests in Sind in 712 to the Mughal emperors – controlled all or part of India from 1193 to the 19th century, when the subcontinent became part of the vast British Empire. When the country won its independence from Britain in 1947, it was split up and the new Muslim state of Pakistan was created. A growing Muslim minority remains in India.

TIMUR'S TOMB
The Mongol war leader Timur (p. 50) was a highly successful soldier who had victories in Iran, India, Syria, and Turkey. When he died in 1405, he was trying to add China to his list of military triumphs. The great wealth he amassed from his conquests is reflected by the rich decoration of his tomb at Samarkand in Central Asia.

FRIDAY MOSQUE, ISFAHAN
Isfahan, Iran, was the capital of the powerful Safavid dynasty (1501–1732), which unified the area and made Shi'i Islam the state religion. The Safavid sultans built a series of stunning buildings in the city, including a large palace complex, several mosques, and the large Friday Mosque. The red-and-blue glazed tilework of the 16th and 17th centuries is in typical Safavid style.

QUTB MINAR, DELHI
In 1193, Afghan ruler Muhammad al-Ghuri conquered northern India. He built a capital at Delhi from which Muslim sultans ruled, putting up buildings like this tall minaret. For the most part, the rule of the Delhi sultans was ended by the campaigns of Timur in 1398–9, but carried on in some areas until 1526.

KHWAJU BRIDGE
One of the achievements of the Safavid dynasty was the construction of the Khwaju Bridge in Isfahan. The bridge is about 440 ft (133 m) long and spans the Zayandeh River with 23 arches. In addition to providing a river crossing, this amazing structure acted as a dam to irrigate the nearby gardens.

Openings allow passersby to enjoy river views in the shade.

The Mughal empire

The Muslim Mughal dynasty ruled in India from 1526 to 1858, with the greatest emperors in power toward the beginning of this period. Under their rule, the diverse Indian subcontinent was united and underwent a unique period of achievement in art, music, literature and architecture. Under the later Mughal rulers, however, the empire began to fall apart.

Babur discusses building progress with his architects

Akbar leads his army into battle

BABUR

The first Mughal emperor was Babur, who came from Iran and was descended from Timur and Genghis Khan. The word Mughal comes from "Mongol," because of Babur's origins. Babur was just 11 when he became a ruler in Transoxiana, and aged 14 when he conquered Samarkand. He established a kingdom in Iran, which he lost, and another in Afghanistan. In 1526, Babur conquered India. A well-educated man, he was a poet and historian who encouraged the arts.

AKBAR

The greatest Mughal emperor was Akbar, who ruled from 1556 to 1605. Skilled in government, Akbar set up an efficient bureaucracy, the structure of which still influences Indian government today. Akbar was also known as one of the most tolerant of rulers. He abolished a tax on the Hindu population, and encouraged artists to combine Hindu and Islamic styles in their work.

AURANGZEB

This book contains the letters of the last important Mughal leader, emperor Aurangzeb (1658–1070), whose rule saw a decline in the health of the Mughal state. He expanded the empire but failed to invest in agriculture and so did not make enough money to support his army or court. He persecuted non-Muslims, taxing Hindus heavily and destroying many of their temples.

China and Southeast Asia

ISLAM HAS BEEN PRACTICED in China since the seventh century when it was introduced to coastal cities by Arab traders. Over the next 200 years, merchants traveling the Silk Road took Islam into the interior. The Muslims of China today are a diverse people descended from many different ethnic groups, including ethnic Chinese, Mongols, and Persians, each with their own customs and cultures. Islam also reached Southeast Asia through trade, and today the largest Muslim population in the world is in Indonesia.

Name of Allah

Outline of bird where wax covered the fabric during dyeing

BY SEA
Some Muslim merchants traveled from the mainland to Southeast Asia in traditional boats with striking curved prows.

BATIK
China and Southeast Asia have always traded in beautiful fabrics, such as silks. This piece has been dyed using the process called batik, which was invented in Java. The dyer applies wax to the parts of the fabric which are to remain uncolored, then soaks the material in dye. When dry, the material is boiled or scraped to remove the wax.

Typical Chinese upward-curving roof

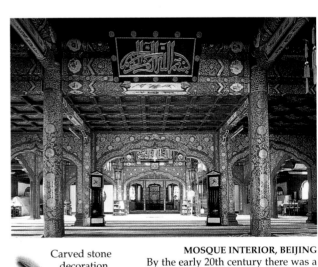

Carved stone decoration from Xi'an mosque

MOSQUE INTERIOR, BEIJING
By the early 20th century there was a sizeable Muslim minority in China. In the larger cities there are lavish mosques like the Niu Jie mosque (above), which has pillars lacquered in black and gold, and walls decorated with both Arabic and Chinese motifs. Most of China's Muslims live in the rural northwestern province of Xinjiang, where the mosques are usually much plainer.

GRAND MOSQUE IN THE CITY OF XI'AN,
When China became communist in 1949, Muslims were given some religious freedom, but during the Cultural Revolution (1966–1976) all religions were outlawed, and mosques were destroyed or closed. In the 1980s, however, many mosques were reopened or rebuilt. China's oldest mosque, the Grand Mosque in Xi'an, can be visited today.

ROD PUPPET

The shadow puppet theater called *wayang golek* is performed with carved and painted wooden figures that are manipulated with rods. *Wayang* is a traditional Javanese entertainment, widely enjoyed by Muslims at festivals and celebrations.

Articulated arm

Wooden rod is used to move puppet's arm.

Clothing conceals stick used to hold puppet.

WEARING THE TUDONG

These schoolgirls from Brunei are wearing the *tudong*, a form of head-covering that extends down to conceal the neck and upper body. Wearing the *tudong* is just one way in which women can obey the Qur'an's instruction to dress modestly (p. 56).

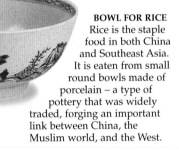

BOWL FOR RICE

Rice is the staple food in both China and Southeast Asia. It is eaten from small round bowls made of porcelain – a type of pottery that was widely traded, forging an important link between China, the Muslim world, and the West.

MIX OF STYLES

This modern mosque in Kuala Kangsar, Malaysia, was built after the country became independent in 1957. This was a good time for Muslims in Malaysia because Islam was recognized as the state's official religion.

MALAYSIAN MOSQUE

Because Islam was brought to Southeast Asia by well-traveled merchants, the area has always been influenced by a mix of cultures. This Malaysian mosque is decorated in the style of mosques in Iran and India.

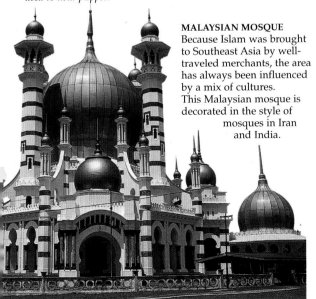

CARAVANSERAI

Merchants traveling by land needed places to stay, so the locals built caravanserais (p. 36) on the routes through Asia to China. In these simple stone buildings, merchants could find a bed and somewhere to stable their camels.

Costume and jewelry

THERE IS NO ONE Muslim style of dress, although the Qur'an instructs women and men to dress modestly. As a result, Muslims wear all types of different clothes, from the traditional garments of the Arabian desert to modern Western dress. A rich variety of traditional costumes is still worn today, particularly on special occasions such as family celebrations. These beautiful garments show how skills such as weaving, dyeing, and embroidery have been refined and handed on from one generation to the next throughout the Islamic world, from North Africa to eastern Asia.

AT SCHOOL
Many Muslim children wear modern dress, like these Chinese children in kindergarten. Only their headgear – the boys' caps and the girls' headdresses – differ from the kinds of clothes worn by children all over the world.

COIN ROBE
In Arabia and western Asia it is an old custom to wear much of your wealth. This Bedouin robe has coins stitched to it. It is made of natural cotton, which is comfortable to wear in the desert heat.

UZBEK BRIDE
In many places, wedding celebrations are a time to put on elaborate traditional costumes. This bride from Uzbekistan wears a gold headdress, a dress of rich fabrics woven with gold threads, and a long embroidered head-covering that falls almost to the floor.

Saudi Arabian woman wearing a face veil

THE VEIL
In some Muslim communities, it is traditional for women to veil their faces. The veil may cover the lower part of the face, up to the eyes, or may cover the whole face, as here.

A MODERN TWIST
Muslim boys often wear this type of brightly colored cap. The shape is traditional, as is the technique of embroidery used to decorate it. But the pattern can be modern, like the helicopter design used here.

GOLD BRACELET
Arab metalworkers pride themselves on their jewelry. For centuries, they worked mostly in silver, but now gold is a popular material for the bracelets and other pieces that are bought for a bride when she marries.

HEAD DECORATION
This is a traditional form of jewelry in the Arabian Peninsula. A woman wears a pair of head decorations, one over each ear.

Chains and roundels made of silver

AMULETS
Some Muslims carry an ornament or piece of jewelry to protect them from evil, called an amulet. This might be a stone carved with a verse from the Qur'an, or a box containing Qur'anic texts.

ENAMELED NECKLACE
Jewelry can be given bright red, blue, and green colors by enameling. This involves applying a mixture of powdered colored glass to the metalwork and heating the piece in a kiln to make the decoration hard and permanent.

CHINESE ROBE
Fine silks, often with added embroidered decoration, are among the most elegant of Chinese traditional garments. The example below has wide sleeves, which are typical of Oriental designs.

DAZZLING DESIGN
This North African robe shows two forms of bright, colorful decoration. The stripes are made by sewing different colored fabrics together. But what really makes the robe stand out is the encrustation of brilliantly colored beads.

TWO-WAY PATTERN
The outside of the Central Asian robe above is produced using the *ikat* technique (p. 35). The lining stands out as its flower patterns contrast well with the zigzag *ikat*.

Islamic society

THE QUR'AN TELLS MUSLIMS that man is God's vice regent on Earth and is responsible for taking good care of everything from the environment to the people around him. Muslims are told to be tolerant of other peoples and to create societies in which justice, personal kindness, and the avoidance of wrongdoing are upheld. Virtues such as these start within the family and the Qur'an describes clearly the roles of men, women, and children. Within these guidelines, which are known as the *sharia*, Muslim society can take a variety of forms.

SULTAN AND HIS SUBJECTS
Muslim countries are governed in different ways. In the past, many had heads of state who ruled with absolute power, like this Moroccan sultan. Since World War II and the abolition of the caliphate (p. 20), most Muslims now live in modern nation states.

SELLING SLAVES
Slavery had been an important part of the social system since ancient times, and was still common in the time of Muhammad. It continued to be a part of life in medieval times as this picture of a North African slave market shows. The Qur'an encouraged the freeing of slaves and insisted that they be treated with kindness.

SCALES OF JUSTICE
Islamic law also covers business, encouraging trade, but setting guidelines that ensure fairness. Since Abbasid times (p. 20), markets in Muslim countries have had officials who checked weights and measures and the quality of merchandise. The *Muhtasib*, as this public official was called, is still found in some traditional markets.

TOLERANCE
The Qur'an stresses that there should be tolerance between Muslims and non-Muslims. Jews and Christians, people who, like Muslims, believe in the One God, are given particular respect in the Qur'an. They should be able to coexist peacefully, like the Muslim and Christian chess-players in this Spanish picture.

"Allah created nothing finer on Earth than justice. Justice is Allah's balance on Earth, and any man who upholds this balance will be carried by Him to Paradise."

THE PROPHET MUHAMMAD

MARCHING TOGETHER
Many Muslims live side by side with people of very different beliefs. For the most part, they live in harmony, like these Muslims and Buddhists in China.

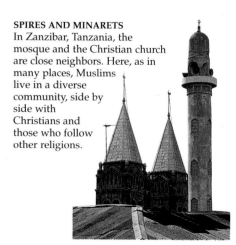

SPIRES AND MINARETS
In Zanzibar, Tanzania, the mosque and the Christian church are close neighbors. Here, as in many places, Muslims live in a diverse community, side by side with Christians and those who follow other religions.

MEN'S ROLE

Islam makes a clear distinction between the roles of men and women in the home. The man's job is to deal with relations between the family and the outside world, as this man is doing when he entertains his guests.

CHILDREN AND FAMILY

Muslims regard children as gifts of Allah and as one of the great joys of life. Parents are expected to care for their children and to give them a good start in life, making sure they have a proper upbringing and education. Children are expected to respect and obey their parents and to show qualities of kindness, virtue, and conscientiousness toward them.

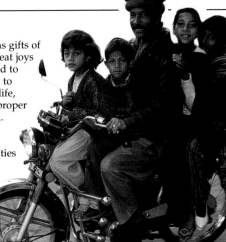

HENNAED HAND

Henna is used in a traditional ritual that is usually performed on the day before a marriage. The bride's hands and feet are adorned with beautiful patterns using a dye made from henna leaves. This may be done by the bride's female friends and relatives.

MARRIED LIFE

Muslims are usually expected to marry and have children. Marriage not only unites individuals, but it also brings together families, making the Muslim community more unified and reflecting the harmony of Allah's creation.

DOWRY BOX

A Muslim man gives his bride-to-be a dowry, a payment in money or property, which may be presented in a box like this. The amount of the dowry can vary according to the man's wealth.

Pattern is said to symbolize strength and love.

WESTERN WOMEN

In many societies, Muslim women are educated to a high level, are employed in professions such as medicine or law, and may even take a prominent part in public life. Baroness Uddin, a Muslim member of the British House of Lords, is a good example.

SUDANESE WOMAN

In traditional Muslim societies such as Sudan, women usually keep to their roles of homemaking and childcare. Even in early Muslim societies, however, there were notable women who worked as scholars and occasionally ruled. Many learned Muslim women, such as the great Egyptian scholar Umm Hani (1376–1466), were famous in the Middle Ages.

Local terra-cotta pot

MAN AT PRAYER

According to Islam, everything comes from Allah and will eventually return to Allah. Qualities that are loved in family members, friends, and the wider society are all qualities that have come from Allah. So the individual's relationship with Allah is paramount. Each Muslim turns to Allah for guidance, forgiveness, and support.

Festivals and ceremonies

THE MUSLIM CALENDAR contains a number of yearly festivals. Some commemorate key events in the history of the faith, such as the birthday of the Prophet or the Night Journey. Others are connected with the Five Pillars of Islam: *'Id al-Adha* (the feast of the sacrifice) takes place during the time of the pilgrimage, and *'Id al-Fitr* marks the end of Ramadan, the month of fasting. There are also festivals such as *Nauruz* in Iran to celebrate the New Year, and celebrations, from birth to marriage, to mark key points in a Muslim's life.

LUNAR CALENDAR
The Islamic calendar is based on the phases of the Moon. Each year has 12 lunar months of 29 or 30 days each, and a total of 354 days. Each month begins with the sighting of the new Moon.

KERBALA
Kerbala, Iraq, is where Muhammad's grandson Husayn was killed in 680. Husayn's shrine (above) is sacred to the Shi'i Muslims, who are the largest religious group in Iran and Iraq. The death of Husayn is marked by the festival of *Ashura* (see opposite).

RAMADAN
During the month of Ramadan, Muslims fast between sunrise and sunset (p.15). At sunset each day, people first pray and then eat. Special lights, such as this star-shaped lantern, may be lit during the evening meal.

MAWLID AN-NABI
These boys from Kenya are taking part in a procession celebrating *Mawlid an-Nabi*, the birthday of the Prophet. This day is a public holiday and is also marked with recitations of a poem called the *Burdah*, in praise of Muhammad.

"EID MUBARAK"
During the festival of *'Id al-Fitr*, people knock on the doors of neighbors, greeting them with the phrase *"Eid Mubarak"* (Blessed *Eid*). Friends or relatives living away are sent *Eid* greeting cards (left).

Eid *greeting card*

Stained glass *panel*

'ID BALLOONS
Colorful balloons are a popular feature of the celebrations of *'Id al-Fitr*, which marks the end of Ramadan (p. 15). Celebrations include a festival prayer, a substantial breakfast, and the giving of alms to the poor.

THE ISLAMIC CALENDAR

MUHARRAM	SAFAR	RABI' AL-AWWAL
The sacred month, 30 days	The month which is void	The first spring
1: *Ra's al-'Am* (New Year)	29 days	30 days
10: *Ashura*		12: Mawlid an-Nabi (birthday of the Prophet)

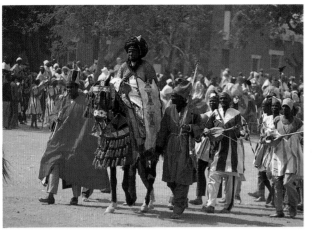

SALLAH FESTIVAL
Some Muslim festivals are local celebrations that take part in just one country or region of the Islamic world. For example, the *Sallah* festival is held in northern Nigeria as part of the rituals marking the end of Ramadan. The highlight is a colorful procession featuring chiefs in ceremonial robes, brightly costumed horsemen, and lute players.

ASHURA
The festival of *Ashura* marks the death of Husayn and, in one of the ceremonies, models of Husayn's tomb are carried through the streets. Plays reenacting the death of Husayn may also be performed.

WHIRLING DERVISH
Members of the Sufi Mevlevi order (p. 35) hold festivals at which they perform their "whirling" dance, known as *sama'*. One such festival marks the death of their founder, the great Sufi poet and mystic, Jalaluddin Rumi (1207–73).

WEDDING CELEBRATIONS
In Islam, a contract of marriage is made by the groom giving the bride-to-be a dowry, and the bride then giving consent to marriage before witnesses. The dowry may be presented in an embroidered wallet. Wedding celebrations vary according to the local traditions of the different areas of the Muslim world, but will usually include recitations from the Qur'an and a great feast.

Dowry wallet

KHITAN
Muslim boys are usually circumcised in a ceremony called *khitan*. This is often done around age seven, though it may be done any time before a boy reaches 12 years old. These Turkish boys are attending a mosque before their *khitan* ceremony.

LAYLAT AL-ISRA' WA'L-MI'RAJ
On the 27th day of the month of *Rajab*, Muslims celebrate Muhammad's Night Journey, when he rode the beast called the *Buraq*, and his Ascension to Heaven (p. 9). This is called *Laylat al-Isra' wa'l-mi'raj*, the Night of the Journey and Ascension.

The Buraq is a "miraculous steed," although depictions of the beast vary.

RABI'ATH-THANI
The second spring
29 days

JUMADA-L-ULA
The first month of dryness
30 days

JUMADA-TH-THANIYYAH
The second month of dryness
29 days

Continued on next page

CANDY TRAY
The availability of sugar meant that many Muslim areas developed their own traditional types of candy. These examples come from Malaysia. Known as *kuch*, they are rich cookies flavored with palm sugar and coconut.

Food

A rich variety of food originated in the Islamic countries, and many of these foods have spread far and wide. This variety is only slightly limited by some simple dietary rules that restrict what a Muslim may eat. Islam forbids the drinking of alcohol, and Muslims are not allowed to eat pork which, as in other traditions, is considered to be unclean. Other animals may be eaten, provided that they are slaughtered in the correct way, with the Name of God pronounced as the creature's life is taken. Meat that is slaughtered in this way is described as *halal*, or lawful to eat.

MINT TEA
Tea is widely drunk in many Muslim countries. Usually served in a glass, hot, sweet mint tea is very popular and refreshing. Lemon tea is a common alternative.

Cardamom

Cumin

Turmeric

SPICES
The spice trade was always important to Muslim merchants, so many spices from India and Southeast Asia found their way into the cooking of the Middle East. Ingredients such as cumin and cardamom were valued for their fragrance, flavor and as aids to digestion.

ON SALE
This mother and daughter in Isfahan, Iran, are buying food from a local dealer in dried fruit and spices. In this traditional shop, most of the goods are displayed loose, so that purchasers can see exactly what they are buying.

FAST FOOD
The idea of fast, ready-to-eat food is nothing new in the Islamic world, and street sellers cooking and selling their own food are a common sight. In Egypt, street vendors like this man sell passersby fava bean patties cooked in the open air and flavored with local herbs.

DATE PALM
Date palms are one of the few crops that grown all over the dry areas of western Asia and northern Africa. Tasty and rich in carbohydrates, dates are a popular staple food.

RAJAB	SHA'BAN	RAMADAN
The revered month	The month of division	Month of great heat
30 days	29 days	30 days
27: *Laylat al-Mi'raj* (Night Journey)	15: *Laylat al-Bara'ah* (memory of the dead – Iran and India)	27: *Laylat al-Qadr* (Night of the Descent of the Qur'an)

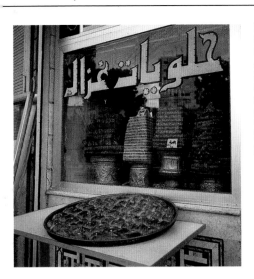

FOR THE SWEET TOOTH
Sweet pastries are one of the delights of western Asia. This shop is in Syria. It is selling local pastries called *hama*, which get their sweetness from a covering of honey. Several different varieties are displayed in the shop window to tempt passersby.

BREADMAKER
Unleavened bread – bread baked without yeast, so that it stays flat and does not rise – is a common staple food throughout the Islamic world. This woman in Kyrgyzstan is making it on an open fire, which is one of the traditional ways to bake bread. Bread like this may also be baked on a hot stone.

ORANGES
Oranges came to Europe along trade routes from the Islamic world, and their juices were quenching thirsts in Western Europe by about the 14th century. The very term orange is derived from the Arabic word *naranj*.

LAMB KEBOBS
The technique of grilling small pieces of meat on a skewer to make a kebob is used in the eastern Mediterranean and Turkey. Kebobs made with ground lamb, cubes of lamb, or pieces of chicken, are now popular all over Europe and beyond.

COFFEE POT
Another item introduced to the West by the Muslims is coffee. Excellent coffee has been grown for centuries in the southwestern corner of the Arabian Peninsula and is still served there today, usually very strong and sweet, from elegant pots like this.

SHARING A MEAL
Hospitality has always been a virtue in Islam, especially in the desert, where food is hard to come by. This early illustration shows some Persians sharing food with a stranger.

FAMILY FOOD
This family in Senegal is cooking their meal over an open fire. When it is ready, they will all eat the food from the one pot. Everyone looks forward to this daily family gathering. It is a chance to catch up on the news as well as to enjoy a welcome meal.

SHAWWAL	DHU L-QA'DAH	DHU L-HIJJAH
The month of hunting	The month of rest	Month of the Pilgrimage
29 days	30 days	29 days (sometimes 30)
1: 'Id al-Fitr (Feast of Fast-breaking)		10: 'Id al-Adha (Feast of Sacrifice)

Index

Acknowledgments

Dorling Kindersley would like to thank: Philip Letsu and Wilfrid Wood for design assistance.

The author would like to thank: Batul Salazar for correcting errors and mistakes of judgment, and for sharing knowledge and sources of information with such generosity and good humor.

Picture Credits
Key: a=above, b=below, c=center, l=left, r=right, t=top; Abbreviations: **BAL:** Bridgeman Art Library, London/New York; **CO:** Christine Osborne; **DKPL:** DK Picture Library; **PS:** Peter Sanders; **C:** Corbis; **RHPL:** Robert Harding Picture Library; **V&A:** Victoria and Albert Museum, London; **SHP:** Sonia Halliday Photographs; **HL:** Hutchison Library; **PP:** Panos Pictures.

1 Ancient Art & Architecture Collection: c. **2 Bodleian Library, University of Oxford:** bc. **BAL:** Giraudon tr; Giraudon/ Topkapi Palace Museum, Istanbul tl. **PS:** tc. **3 AKG London:** bl. **C:** tl. **DKPL:** Glasgow Museums br. **CO:** c. **4 BAL:** cr, crb, bc; Stapleton Collection cr. **Werner Forman Archive:** crb. **Sanderson:** bl. **5 DKPL:** Ashmolean tr. **6 C:** Araldo de Luca br; Paul Almasy bl. **DKPL:** British Museum tl. **PS:** cl. **Photograph by Paul Lunde:** tr. **7 C:** Archivio Iconografico br. **DKPL:** British Museum tr. **8 DKPL:** British Museum tl. **Impact Photos:** Alan Keohane cr. **Salazar:** bl. **PS:** cl, bc. **9 AKG London:** British Museum, London br. **Salazar:** bl. **10 Ancient Art & Architecture Collection:** tl. **BAL:** Musee Conde, Chantilly, France: 10-11. **DKPL:** British Library cl, bl. **11 DKPL:** Ashmolean tr;

British Library cr; Glasgow Museum cr. **Private Collection:** bl. **12 BAL:** Stapleton collection tl, bc. **PS:** cl. **13 DKPL:** National Maratime Museum tc. **PS:** c, c, cr, cr, bl. **Private Collection:** tr. **14 Photograph by Alexander Stone Lunde:** cr. Private Collection: bl. **15 AKG London:** cr. **HL:** John Egan br. **PS:** cl. **Nomad, King's Parade, Cambridge:** tr. **16 Private Collection:** tl. **PS:** bl (both) 16-17 **V&A:** cr. **17 BAL:** Inistitute of Oriental Studies, St Petersburg, Russia bc. **Salazar:** bl. **Photograph by Paul Lunde:** br. **18 CO:** br. **Private Collection:** tl. **Photograph by Alexander Stone Lunde:** tr. **19 BAL:** tc. **CO:** cr. **V&A:** tr. **20 BAL:** Kunsthistorisches Meseum, Vienna, Austria br; Stapleton Collection bl. **DKPL:** Ashmolean c; **British Museum:** 20-21. **21 AKG London:** br. **BAL:** Le Tresor de L@Abbaye de Saint-Maurice, France tl; Stapleton Collection bl. **PS:** cb. **V&A:** tr. **22 Photograph by Paul Lunde:** bl. **C:** Roger Wood br. **The Art Archive:** Archaeological Museum, Madrid tl. **SHP:** Jane Taylor cl. **Impact Photos:** Jerry Flynn cr. **23 BAL:** Volubilis, Morocco tl. Monasterio de El Escorial, Spain bl. **C:** Archivo Iconografico tr. **Archivo Fotgrafico:** br. **24 BAL:** bl; Louvre, Paris cr; Museo Real Academia de Medicina, Madrid tr. **CO:** br. **25 BAL:** bl; Topkapi Palace Museum, Istanbul, Turkey br. **CO:** cr. **Private Collection:** tl, tr. **26 BAL:** British Library, London tr. **C:** Adam Woolfit br. British Museum bl. 26-27 **RHPL:** David Beatty tl. **27 BAL:** Royal Asiastic Society, London bc. **DKPL:** British Library tl. **Mary Evans Picture Library:** br. **V&A:** tr. **28 Bodleian Library, University of Oxford:** c. **BAL:** British Library tr. **CO:** bl. **29 BAL:** Topkapi Palace Museum, Istanbul, Turkey br; University Library,

Istanbul, Turkey tl. **DKPL:** National Maritime Museum cr. **CO:** tr. **30 BAL:** Bibliotheque Nationale, Paris, France tl; Eton College, Windsor cr; Institute of Oriental Studies, St Petersburg, Russia bl. **DKPL:** Science Museum br. **31 DKPL:** Museum of the Royal Pharmaceutical Society cb; Science Museum r. **Werner Forman Archive:** ct; Oriental Collection, State University Library, Leiden tl. **James Stone Lunde:** br. **32 BAL:** tr. **C:** Abbie Enock: Travel Ink cl; Charles and Josette Lenars 32-33. **CO:** cr. **PS:** tl. **33 DKPL:** Barnabas Kindersley cl. **34 Ahuzan Gallery, Ahuzan Islamic Art, London:** c. BAL: tr. **DKPL:** Aditya Patankar bl. **John Gillow:** br. **35 Bodleian Library, University of Oxford:** cl. **DKPL:** Glasgow Museum br. **BAL:** Egyptian National Library, Cairo, Egypt cr. **36 Panos Pictures:** D. Sanson c. Private Collection: clb. **37 BAL:** British Library, London tl. **SHP:** 1840 Engraving by Thomas Allom, hand painted by Laura Lushington cl. **CO:** r. **38 BAL:** Institute of Oriental Studies, St. Petersberg, Russia tr. **DKPL:** National Maritime Museum 38-39; Royal Museum of Scotland cl. **Mary Evans Picture Library:** tl. **CO:** bl. **39 DKPL:** David Gower tc. **SHP:** Topkapi Palace Museum cr. **PS:** tr. **40 DKPL:** British Library cr; Natural History Museum tr; Pitt Rivers Museum bl. **CO:** tr. **Property of Nomad, Kings Parade, Cambridge:** c. John Gillow: cb. **41 James Stone Lunde:** tr. **42 BAL:** Bibliotheque Nationale tl; Bibliotheque nationale, Paris cl. **C:** Dave G.Houser b. **43 AKG London:** tr. **BAL:** Bonhams, London br; British Library, London cr; BritishLibrary, London bc. **C:** 44 **DKPL:** Arbour Antiques 44-45; Pitt Rivers Museum c. **SHP:** tl. **Photograph by Alexander Stone Lunde:** bl. **V&A:** c, 44-45. **45 BAL:** tc; Bargello Museum, Florence l. **James Stone Lunde:** cla. **46 BAL:** Louvre, Paris, France cr;

Monasterio de El Escorial, Spain c. **C:** Adam Woolfit tr; John Hesleltine 46-47. **DKPL:** British Museum tl. **47 Archivo Fotografico:** br. **C:** cl; Edifice bc; Michael Busselle tr; Ric Ergenbright tl. **47 HL:** Juliet Highet c. **48 AKG London:** c. **CO:** tl. **PP:** Marcus Rose 48-49. **O. Clasen:** tr, **Paul Lunde:** bl. **49 C:** Gerard Degeorge tr. **DKPL:** Pavillion Musem and Art Galleries tl. **Fotomas Index:** cr. **PS:** cl, br. **50 AKG London:** tl. **BAL:** cl, br; British Museum bl. **51 BAL:** tr, bl. **The Art Archive:** Topkapi Musuem, Istanbul br. **SHP:** c. **52 C:** Paul Almasy b; Sheldan Collins cr. **DKPL:** Ashmolean Museum tl. **RHPL:** cl, c. **53 AKG London:** V&A tr, cl. **54 CO:** tl. **John Gillow:** cr, bl, bc. **55 C:** Janet Wishnetsky br. **RHPL:** David Holdsworth tr. **CO:** bl. **PS:** cr. **James Stone Lunde:** tl. **Private Collection:** c. **56 RHPL:** F Jack Jackson l. **PS:** tr, bc. 56-57 **Property of Nomad, Kings Parade, Cambridge:** c (robes and hat). **57 Sudhir Kasilwal:** cr. **Property of Nomad, Kings Parade, Cambridge:** tl. **58 BAL:** Biblioteca Monasterio del Escorial, Madrid, Spain cr; Bibliotheque Nationale, Paris c. **C:** Earl & Nazima Kowall bl. **SHP:** tl. **Panos Pictures:** Marc Schlossman br. **Science Photo Library:** Erich Schrempp tr. **59 RHPL:** Bruno Morandi c; David Poole br. **PP:** Clive Shirley tl; Liba Taylor bl; Piers Benatar tr. **Salazar:** cr. **PS:** cl. **Baroness Udin/Universal Pictorial Press:** clb. **60 CO:** tr, cb. **PS:** c, br. **Property of Nomad, King's Parade, Cambridge:** br. **61 RHPL:** Adam Woolfit cl; J H C Wilson tr. **HL:** cl. **PP:** Mark McEvoy bl. **Property of John Gillow:** cr. **Collection Ali Bellagha:** br. **62 A-Z Botanical Collection:** Matt Johnston bl. **PP:** Trygve Bolstad cr. **63 BAL:** British Library, London bl. **DKPL:** David Murray & Jules Selmes cl. **RHPL:** Christopher Rennie tl. **HL:** Sarah Errington tr. **James Stone Lunde:** c. **PP:** Jeremy Hartley br.